Leaving Prostitution

Getting Out and Staying Out of Sex Work

Sharon S. Oselin

NEW YORK UNIVERSITY PRESS
New York and London

NEW YORK UNIVERSITY PRESS
New York and London
www.nyupress.org

References to Internet websites (URLs) were accurate at the time of writing.
Neither the author nor New York University Press is responsible for URLs that
may have expired or changed since the manuscript was prepared.

Library of Congress Cataloging-in-Publication Data

Oselin, Sharon S.
Leaving prostitution : getting out and staying out of sex work / Sharon S. Oselin.
pages cm
Includes bibliographical references and index.
ISBN 978-0-8147-8588-1 (cloth : alk. paper)
ISBN 978-0-8147-7037-5 (pbk. : alk. paper)
1. Prostitution--United States. 2. Prostitutes--Rehabilitation--. 3. Prostitutes--
Services for--United States. I. Title.
HQ144.O84 2014
363.4'40973--dc23
                                2013045556

New York University Press books are printed on acid-free paper,
and their binding materials are chosen for strength and durability.
We strive to use environmentally responsible suppliers and materials
to the greatest extent possible in publishing our books.

Manufactured in the United States of America
c 10 9 8 7 6 5 4 3 2 1
p 10 9 8 7 6 5 4 3 2 1

Also available as an ebook

For Matthew, and my parents

CONTENTS

ACKNOWLEDGMENTS

First and foremost, I sincerely thank the women immersed within these prostitute-serving organizations (PSOs) who made this book possible. Most were very receptive to my presence and eagerly participated in this research project. Despite the magnitude of their own challenges and struggles, they took time to speak with me, candidly revealed their experiences (even traumatic and painful ones), and divulged extremely personal information to a virtual stranger. That in and of itself took courage and strength. I applaud the fortitude these individuals exhibited during their transition off the streets, as the foray into the unchartered territory of a new life is a daunting task.

I must also acknowledge the generosity of the PSOs and their staff members who allowed me access to conduct research at their respective programs. Not only did these staff members treat me with kindness and respect, they freely offered their time to answer my questions, showed me around, and supported my study in a myriad of ways. In particular, I want to thank Denise H. for being so hospitable to me during my fieldwork. Overall, I admire how deeply invested the staff members are in the well-being and success of those they serve. It was extremely touching to witness.

My first sociological mentor, Michael Skladany, inspired me by his enthusiastic teaching while at Michigan State University. I may not have made it to graduate school without his encouragement. The support, guidance, and intellect of my advisors and colleagues helped vastly improve this project at each stage along the way. The academic work of my advisors at the University of California, Irvine exemplified high-quality and compelling sociological research, which set the bar for performance quite high. In particular, I thank David Snow for challenging me to become a more thoughtful sociologist, for posing hard questions about my work when needed, and for his unwavering faith in this project and my ability to successfully complete it. Calvin Morrill likewise provided support for this project, showed consistent enthusiasm about it, and regularly brainstormed ideas with me in his office. I always trusted Valerie Jenness to give honest feedback about my work, which was invaluable, and she always managed to do so in a constructive manner. I sought her out for practical advice on countless occasions and I appreciate her willingness to do so. Finally, Jen'nan Ghazal Read showed me how to code, analyze, and write up qualitative data, and was readily available to dispense guidance and suggestions when asked. I would not possess the skill set I have today, integral to this project and book, without the help of these mentors.

Fellow scholars of sex work Ron Weitzer, Barb Brents, and Jody Miller have read and commented on ideas in this book and various portions of it. They candidly shared their experiences with book publishing, their proposals, and offered counsel throughout this process. I am very grateful for their support.

Many colleagues and friends have provided emotional support and encouragement over the years, including Goldie Komaie, Steve Boutcher, Becky Trammell, Christine Oh, Danielle Rudes, Yuki Kato, and Kelsy Kretschmer. I will never forget the countless coffees, lunches, and conversations that sustained me and spurred me on to complete this book. Catherine Corrigall-Brown, Jody Agius Vallejo, and Katja Guenther were especially helpful by sharing their experiences with book publishing, providing useful tips, and overall reminding me of the value of my work and its contribution. I appreciate all my colleagues at California State University, Los Angeles, who expressed interest in my book and who work so hard to build our department and better serve our students. Elaine Draper, in particular, was a relentless cheerleader of this book, even long before its acceptance.

I received financial support from UC Irvine's Center for Organizational Research (COR), UC Irvine, CSU Los Angeles, and the American Association of University Women (AAUW) that enabled me to conduct fieldwork in various cities and to analyze and write portions of this manuscript. This monetary and symbolic support encouraged me and motivated me over the years.

I appreciate the hard work of the NYU editors, and especially Ilene Kalish, for believing in this project and walking me through the publishing process. I thank the anonymous reviewers for their time and recommendations for improvement. Altogether, their thoughtful feedback and comments on various drafts vastly improved the quality of the manuscript.

Many of my dear family members and friends encouraged my work and career in so many small and large ways. They continue to bring much joy into my life, and for that I am grateful. I feel so fortunate for my friend Heather, who is also an academic. We've come a long way together over the years. Jamie is always one of the first people to sing my praises and point out my accomplishments. Jennifer distracts me with amusing stories that bring a smile to my face. Amanda, Diane, and Veronica help me be the person I strive to be. John and Elaine Novak are the coolest and most generous relatives one could ask for, and Rich, Karen, and Nolan Oselin enrich my life by their very existence.

I am lucky to have such amazing parents, who have been relentless supporters, both emotionally and financially, over the years. They taught me an ethic of hard work and to be generous and gracious to others. I cannot adequately express my gratitude for Matthew, who distracted me when I needed it most, read various drafts of this book, and provided another perspective when I was stuck in a rut. I am beyond thankful for his adventurous spirit, keen intellect, love, and unwavering support.

1

Introduction

Leaving the Tricks and the Trade

Marquietta, a middle-aged African American woman, worked in prostitution for over 15 years in a large midwestern city. She was a woman with a sweet disposition and quick to help others, but was rather quiet and withdrawn in social settings. When talking one-on-one, however, she opened up and candidly recalled the events in her life bookended by her entrance and exit from sex work. Her first paid sex act occurred when she worked in customer service at a local paper. She sold sex to her manager and used the income to purchase drugs. When she was eventually terminated from her job because she neglected to show up to work after a two-day bender—ironically fired by this same manager—she moved to Atlanta with her husband and three children in order to be closer to her relatives. While living in Atlanta, her marriage became strained, largely due to her struggles with addiction. She ultimately separated from her husband, after which she experienced a mental breakdown and was admitted to a hospital for treatment.

Upon release, Marquietta told her husband she needed time to adjust to her new circumstances and could not live with him in the interim. She temporarily moved in with a friend; her husband reacted to this decision by moving back to Chicago with their children. Experiencing feelings of abandonment, she wanted to return to her husband and children but could not afford the trip. Her relatives would not loan her the funds because she was still using drugs, and she ultimately felt that selling sex was the only way to acquire the money. Marquietta initially hooked up with a truck driver who was on his way north, but he left her stranded in a motel after their tryst. She then sought out another trucker and had sex with him in exchange for a ride north. It was in this way that she managed to arrive back in Chicago, hoping to reunite with her family.

After a brief reunion with her family, Marquietta's life changed dramatically. The attempt she made to restore her marriage was both dramatic and short-lived, because she could not remain sober. Her husband kicked her out of the house, her drug addiction escalated after she left, and she began to work regularly as a street prostitute to support her habit. I inquired about her emotional state during this time period. When Marquietta recalled the very first trick she turned on the streets, her most salient emotion was terror. But she also said that this feeling subsided after a few encounters, after which sex work felt like "easy money." Marquietta conceded that it became increasingly difficult to effectively "turn off" her emotions during sexual trysts, and she eventually began to wrestle with difficult moral questions about who she was, what she did, and how she was raised. She often felt embarrassed and demeaned due to neighborhood gossip and stigma. But, as many street prostitutes attest, drugs were an effective means to temporarily stymie the flood of negative emotions.

Years went by, and Marquietta started to seriously contemplate leaving prostitution permanently—a decision reinforced by a handful of her regular clients who advised her to quit because she was "worth more than that."[1] Buttressed by a growing fear that sex work (and the interrelated drug use) would take her life, these words of encouragement resonated with her. Indeed, her fear of violence and death were exacerbated by the increased brutality she witnessed on the streets—five prostitutes she knew well were found dead in garbage cans during this time period. Her former roommate and coprostitute's lifeless body was found rolled up in a carpet behind a restaurant in an area they worked together.

These experiences coalesced in an existential crisis that Marquietta tackled by entering a drug treatment center. She felt that if she could quit using drugs, then she could stop working on the streets. After multiple failed stints in rehab, however, she was not quite ready for such a drastic change. She explained, "I knew I needed to quit in my head but I did not yet feel it in my heart." She believed that drugs and sex work held a powerful physical, mental, and spiritual grasp over her.

A few years later, she ended up serving a five-month sentence in jail due to drug and prostitution charges. While incarcerated she solicited the help of New Horizons, a program that conducts outreach to prostitutes in jails and penitentiaries to encourage them to enroll in their program upon release and leave prostitution altogether. New Horizons accepted her, but she changed her mind and decided not to enter the program after she completed her sentence and instead moved in with a man she knew. The relationship quickly soured after only a few months, due to his drug and alcohol use, while Marquietta struggled to remain sober. She finally left him and moved in with her sister.

Again, things took a turn for the worse, and she realized she needed to make a radical lifestyle change. She described it as a moment of clarity that broke through the haze of her desolate life: "I went to my sister's and when things got desperate for me, I remembered that I interviewed with New Horizons back when I was in jail, and I was accepted. And they already told me if I ever needed to come back in the future that I could. That's what I did." So she reached out to them at a point in her life when she felt that New Horizons was her last chance, and perhaps the only way to avoid a tragic ending to her life. Marquietta had just completed five months in New Horizons when I first met her.

Research on Street Prostitution

I spent the last 10 years researching female street prostitutes, specifically those affiliated with organizations that provide services to them, which I call prostitute-serving organizations (PSOs).[2] Throughout this time, I had the opportunity to spend countless hours interacting with these women and engaging them in conversations within multiple US cities. My sample is comprised exclusively of female prostitutes.[3] As a result, when I refer to prostitutes throughout this book, I discuss females who engage in street-level sex work.

Typically when I have conversations with others about my research one of the first questions they ask is: "Why do they do it?" And it is usually women, both within academia and outside it, who insist there *must* be other options. Even a cursory assessment of the extensive research on female sex workers unequivocally provides the most obvious explanation: They do it for the money. While this answer is too simplistic, and I discuss alternative explanations in chapter 2, there is ample scholarly support that these individuals indeed tend to have limited career options.[4] One colleague challenged this assumption when she remarked, "Why don't they work at McDonald's, where they aren't breaking the law and don't need a degree?" In *Nickel and Dimed*, seasoned journalist Barbara Ehrenreich explores the feasibility of this statement by documenting the difficulties of survival on the income generated from low-wage jobs. While those who perform street-level sex work experience heightened risks that low-wage workers do not, they also have the potential to make a lot more money. Certain researchers even argue that working in prostitution is a very rational (rather than irrational) decision for those who come from lower socioeconomic statuses and backgrounds.[5]

Although estimates indicate that street prostitutes comprise only a small proportion of sex workers overall, many studies show that this population is likely the most disadvantaged group.[6] Social science research reveals that street prostitutes endure exceptionally high rates of physical and sexual abuse at the hands of clients, pimps (men who "manage" prostitutes), and police.[7] Moreover, street prostitutes are among the most likely to be arrested by law enforcement due to their heightened visibility, and may even comprise as high as 80 to 90 percent of total prostitution arrests.[8] Beyond involvement in the criminal justice system, drug use may heighten risks of the trade, a phenomenon that appears to be widespread among street working prostitutes.[9] Drug use pulls some women into the trade, while for others it intensifies after their entrance, as it becomes a coping mechanism. This was certainly the case for Marquietta. One report, from the US Department of Justice, concluded that 92 percent of women in prostitution regularly used drugs or alcohol.[10] These trends are corroborated by my sample, where every woman except one admitted to a drug addiction that coincided with her tenure in sex work.

In light of these factors, those who research sex workers continue to debate the status of women within this industry: Are they victims of a patriarchal system forced to sell their bodies, a position commonly called the *oppression paradigm*, or are they women who use their sexuality for profit and derive benefits from this engagement, a stance known as the *empowerment paradigm*?[11] A third perspective, the *polymorphous paradigm*, argues that sex workers fall along a continuum of victimization and empowerment given their personal circumstances, experiences, and working conditions.[12]

Finally, I must acknowledge a burgeoning area of research related to sex work—sex trafficking—usually concentrated on women and minors. This topic garners much attention and generates debates across public, legal, and academic spheres. As defined by the Trafficking Victims Protection Act (TVPA) of 2000, sex trafficking is "the recruitment, harboring, transportation, provision, or obtaining of a person for the purpose of a commercial sex act." When coercion is involved with adults or the person is a minor and induced to engage in sex acts, this constitutes trafficking in the eye of the law. Most practitioners and scholars tend to view sex trafficking from an oppression stance, especially when it comes to minors and young women. None of the women included in this book report being trafficked into sex work. However, one could make a case that some fit the criteria described above regarding enticement or inducement by male adults. I will revisit this issue again in chapter 2 when I discuss initial entrance into prostitution.

In this book, I do not endorse a particular paradigm and thereby relegate all prostitutes into that category, but rather aim to explore the careers of street prostitutes with a particular focus on their exits from the trade. To that end, I want the women's stories and words to depict their experiences rather than simply assign an overarching status (e.g., oppressed or empowered) unto them. Although their backgrounds, motivations, and goals varied, the work-related experiences across these four samples were strikingly similar.

Pathways Out of Sex Work

The negative experiences affiliated with street-level prostitution—such as arrests, drug addiction, lack of support networks, and stigma—can make exiting even more arduous. Conversely, for some women, these very factors can serve as an impetus to leave the trade. While the transition out of sex work is an underresearched topic, some recent theoretical headway has been made on certain related aspects. Family studies scholar Rochelle Dalla concludes that women exit prostitution via three main avenues: jail, on their own, and via prostitute-serving organizations.[13] A few studies examine female prostitutes' motivations for leaving the trade and unearth the following reasons: health crises, hitting bottom, experiencing life-changing events, regaining custody of their kids, the changing street-level subculture of prostitution, and spiritual awakening.[14]

Scholars who focus on exits from sex work note the need for further investigation of this process.[15] As social scientists Baker, Dalla, and Williamson summarize, "Few studies have focused solely on this process or described it within any formal conceptual framework."[16] There are a few important empirically based contributions that should be acknowledged. Social workers Månsson and Hedin developed a five-stage model that comprised exiting among prostitutes: *drifting in, ensnarement, prebreakaway, breakaway*, and *after the breakaway*.[17] This model draws attention to specific structural, relational, and individual factors that facilitate the transition out of sex work. Moreover, Baker, Dalla, and Williamson also formulated an integrated six-stage model of exiting prostitution that includes *immersion, awareness, deliberate planning, initial exit, reentry*, and *final exit*.[18] Despite these studies, academics have limited understanding of the social-psychological stages of change that occur for individuals who move through this process and how contextual factors influence it.

Analogous areas of research can help shed light on this transition. For instance, criminological studies on desistance—analyses of how and why individuals cease their engagement in criminal activities—are applicable. Two well-known scholars in this field are criminologists John Laub and

Robert Sampson. In numerous publications, they analyze data on male offenders over multiple time points and find that turning points in the life cycle and the associated informal social control mechanisms (e.g., marriage, children, and military service) engender social bonds that promote desistance from crime.[19]

The preceding studies are derived exclusively from male subjects, and therefore illuminate why and how *men* cease to commit crimes. However, they raise the question of whether the desistance process varies by the gender of the offender. Indeed, scholars interested in gender and crime lament the overall dearth of research that focuses on female offenders. In the past few decades, feminist criminologists have started to address this gap in their work.[20] Yet it is still unclear whether long-standing desistance theories based upon male subjects similarly apply to female offenders. In an effort to further this line of inquiry, sociologists Peggy Giordano and colleagues find that traditional attachments, such as marriage or job stability, are not strongly linked to desistance among female offenders.[21] Instead, their research indicates that female desistance is tied to the following social psychological changes: a basic openness to change, exposure to particular "hooks of change," envisioning a new self, and transformation away from the viability or relevance of the deviant lifestyle.[22] In her recent book, *Legacies of Crime: A Follow-Up of the Children of Highly Delinquent Girls and Boys*, Peggy Giordano stresses that social learning and social controls likewise impact desistance from crime.[23]

Despite these inroads, this process may unfold differently according to specific types of offenders. Rather than lump all female offenders into one homogeneous group, based on the assumption that they share uniform experiences, it may be more fruitful to explore desistance as it occurs among particular groups of offenders. Prostitution is an activity that garners significant social and legal attention, and therefore, those involved in it are often classified and treated as a distinct population. Research carried out by Månsson and Hedin, and Baker, Dalla, and Williamson, referenced above, begins to examine how prostitutes experience this transition.

Those who study desistance also note that successful role transitions sustain it.[24] Social roles are noteworthy because they provide a vantage point for understanding the world, and they inform human behaviors. Individuals take on numerous roles throughout their lives and transition from one role to another over the life course, a phenomenon referred to as *role exiting*. Social psychologist Jenna Howard claims most research tends to focus on the socialization and internalization of new roles but neglects the overall exiting process.[25] One of the major exceptions to this pattern is found in the work by sociologist Helen Rose Ebaugh, whose book examines the stages that comprise role exits for those leaving a variety of social roles.[26] Her study reveals the four stages integral to this process: first doubts, the seeking and weighing of alternatives, turning points, and establishing an ex-role identity. Ebaugh's theoretical framework is a useful point of departure for this analysis of prostitutes' transitions out of sex work. My book, however, extends her study in two significant ways. First, I focus on those immersed within a fairly gendered role, one that is also highly deviant and criminal. These features distinguish it from other roles, given the stigma, criminalization, and low status attached to it, all of which are amplified for females. Second, I carry out a comparative exploration of how contexts—organizations—shape the exiting process and the stages of change that correspond to it.

Social roles are also significant, as they are intricately related to identity formation. Social psychologists claim that the roles individuals occupy exert great influence over their identity, and therefore a role exit is likely to cultivate an identity transformation.[27] As society designates certain roles deviant or criminal, the role, for those who occupy it, tends to become especially salient for the individual and therefore overshadows other concurrent roles and associated identities for him or her. When labeled individuals attempt to leave such roles, they often experience greater difficulty due to the lingering effects of stigmatization.[28] In rare cases, individuals can capitalize on their former deviant role and use it to secure a conventional one. Sociologist J. David Brown illustrates this phenomenon in his study on former addicts who used their past role as qualification for their new career role of substance abuse counselor.[29] This practice is atypical among street prostitutes, given that there are few opportunities where sex worker credentials translate into other legal professional roles. Accordingly, sociologist Teela Sanders finds former prostitutes tend to conceal their past history of sex work in order to avoid negative repercussions.[30]

Organizational Culture and Individual Change

This comparative study analyzes how women exit street prostitution while immersed within prostitute-serving organizations. Federal, state, and local governments dedicate few resources to assist exits from prostitution, and as a result, nonprofit organizations fill a niche that would otherwise remain vacant. PSOs provide services and distribute resources to prostitutes with the intention of improving the quality of their lives. And, although they have a common purpose, they also develop unique program cultures while working toward their goals. As sex workers become affiliated with a particular PSO, they are exposed to its culture and are often influenced by it.

Labor studies scholar Gideon Kunda investigates organizational culture at a corporate setting in his book, *Engineering Culture*.[31] In doing so, he identifies the various control mechanisms that influence members, which he calls coercive or normative. Coercive control is formally maintained by organizational sanctions, rewards, and punishments that operate as incentives to prompt particular actions among members. In contrast, normative control mechanisms direct individuals by informally shaping the underlying experiences, thoughts, and feelings that guide their actions. When internalized by members, normative practices, rather than coercive strategies, seem to better engender thoughts and actions that help sustain an organizational culture.

Organizational scholars claim that forces of controls are inherent to the organizational socialization process.[32] However, the effectiveness of this member socialization is contingent upon the organizational attributes and the dynamics that unfold within these confines.[33] Total institutions, for instance, may cultivate and enforce control mechanisms much more than other types of organizations because they rely on member compliance and obedience to run smoothly. Other types of settings, such as therapeutic programs, tend to promote member autonomy and self-direction, and therefore are less likely to implement control mechanisms. The organizational cultures rife with control mechanisms engender a power-laden dynamic between the staff and members, where the former pushes the latter to internalize and adopt prescribed values, behaviors, and goals. Social science research repeatedly demonstrates that organizationally based control mechanisms indeed have the ability to affect a member's role and identity.[34]

In this book I address the following questions that center on role transitions, organizational cultures, and the dynamic between the two by employing a comparative analysis of four PSOs: What is the process of role exiting for female sex workers, and are there phases that indicate such a transition? How do PSOs, and their members, facilitate or constrain this process among prostitutes? What factors sustain role exits as women leave a PSO?

Prelude to the Study

When I initially began this project in 2002, I wanted to research street-level prostitutes. However, I did not know how to gain access to this population. I turned to the Internet and searched using the keywords "prostitutes" and "Southern California" to see what opportunities for research existed locally. After only a few clicks, I found a website that featured a program designed to help women in prostitution within commuting distance from me. While I was aware of homeless shelters and drug treatment centers, I had no idea that organizations existed to specifically aid prostitutes. I called the program, spoke with the director, and quickly gained access to conduct research at this prostitute-serving organization.[35] As I began fieldwork at this site, the topic of exiting and how it unfolds for individuals immersed within PSOs struck me as especially intriguing. It ultimately became the focus of this book.

Study Design, Sampling, and Data Collection

A short time later, when I wanted to extend this study, I realized I did not know much about PSOs nationally and could not answer the most basic questions about them: How many are there? Is there much variation across

Table 1.1 Prostitute-Serving Organizations by US Region

East	6
Midwest	9
South	3
SouthWest	2
West	9
	N=29

programs? Where are they located? Because I was unable to locate any comprehensive detailed information on these programs, I began to collect this data as a first step in this larger project. This task became the initial phase of my research design, which consisted of the following: (1) compiling the names and contact information of all the domestic PSOs, (2) conducting phone interviews with a PSO representative from each site in order to collect basic program information, and (3) based on this data, completing ethnographic research at four strategically selected PSOs to ensure study comparability. As a result, I was able to triangulate my methods because I implemented multiple data collection techniques.[36] To assess the range of PSOs I used snowball sampling tactics, coupled with Internet searches, and located 29 prostitute-serving organizations within the United States.[37] Table 1.1 shows these results by listing the frequency of PSOs according to region.

I attempted to gather information from as many PSOs as possible via phone interviews with one staff member per program, which ultimately resulted in 21 program representative interviews between 2002 and 2003. My access to interviews and information on these organizations was not without its trials and tribulations, and I met with a variety of reactions from their gatekeepers—rudeness, secrecy, no response, guarded suspicion, openness, trust, and a genuine interest in my work. The interviews (most often with program directors) focused on questions about the program history, staff, services offered, clients, funding, philosophy, goals, networks, and outreach. The remaining eight PSOs either chose not to participate or did not respond to my repeated attempts to contact them.

The interview results indicated that PSOs were extremely varied along numerous dimensions, such as their duration of existence, modes of client entrée, structure, location, services, number of staff members, funding, and so on. For instance, half of the PSOs offered residential treatment for prostitutes that consisted of three months or more, approximately one-quarter provided temporary shelter (less than three months), and the remaining quarter ran drop-in shelters, held support groups, or offered educational classes for prostitutes.

During this period, I was not only in the midst of fieldwork at Phoenix in Los Angeles but was also simultaneously conducting phone surveys of PSOs nationwide. After I reviewed the characteristics of the other sites, based upon my phone interview data, I picked three additional PSOs where I intended to conduct future ethnographies: New Horizons in Chicago, Illinois; Safe Place in Minneapolis, Minnesota; and Seeds in Hartford, Connecticut.[38] I selected these particular sites due to their variation in terms of modes of client entrée, organizational structure, program duration, and region (see the appendix for in-depth descriptions of these programs). I was specifically interested in these factors because previous research on people-processing organizations emphasized their importance.[39] Not all of these factors end up being relevant to my final analysis; however, I initially operated on the premise that each had the potential to influence my findings. Despite some overlap across sites, the four PSOs reflect the diversity of these organizations and enable comparisons across programs. Table 1.2 illustrates the variation of the programs I selected for ethnographic investigation.

Table 1.2 Variations among Selected Prostitute-Serving Organizations

	Modes of Entree	Org. Structure	Time	City
New Horizons	Both	Total institution	1.5 – 2 years	Chicago, IL
Phoenix	Both	Total institution	1.5 – 2 years	Los Angeles, CA
Safe Place	Both	Quasi-total instit.	3 months	Minneapolis, MN
Seeds	Involuntary	Day program	2 weeks	Hartford, CT

Gaining research access to PSOs can be a challenging task as most are quasi-private—meaning that gatekeepers often grant admission to outsiders based upon that individual's possession of certain credentials or attributes.[40] I believe it was my relationship and experience working with Phoenix, a long-standing program, coupled with my academic credentials, that opened doors for me to conduct research at the other three PSOs.

Ethnographic Methodology

Since exiting prostitution is a process-oriented research question, I conducted ethnographic research at PSOs in order to observe, converse with, and interview individuals at these sites to address it. I collected in-depth qualitative data at four organizations that directly work with prostitutes, a comparative case study approach that was comprised of not only four PSOs but also four samples of prostitutes and staff. This strategy allowed me to access this population and also provided insight into the organizational culture at each site. The "thick description" ethnographies illuminate the contextually embedded details and interactions within these sites over time, which allows for modest generalizations to be drawn about exiting processes.[41] The interviews were purposive in that I targeted street prostitutes and PSO staff members. I utilized a grounded theory approach for this project, where the concepts and understandings emerged from the data rather than being developed prior to data collection and then tested.[42]

In this second stage of my data collection I was immersed within each site for approximately three months, where I worked as an intern and known researcher. I visited each organization between three and five days per week for the duration of this time and typically stayed between six and eight hours per visit. Ethnography consisted of the following tasks: observation and semistructured interviews with female prostitutes; observation of interactions between clients, clients and staff members, and staff members; and observation and semistructured interviews with staff members.

This strategy enabled me to employ both a top-down and bottom-up approach in order to examine PSOs and the individuals affiliated with them. Within each setting I observed the staff, identified and assessed the organizational goals, noted how the staff attempted to implement goals and rules, recorded staff interactions with clients, and observed whether workers enforced program rules. I also observed the prostitutes who utilized these services, how they responded to the staff members and program rules, how they interacted with one another, and their overall verbal and behavioral changes over time. My duties at each site included teaching occasional classes to the clients, generating reports for program directors, and providing feedback to the program staff members. In addition, I was able to observe group classes and staff meetings, as well as engage in small talk and one-on-one conversations with the staff and clients while they were doing mundane everyday activities—smoking, gossiping, doing homework, paperwork, household tasks, or preparing and eating meals.

On top of keeping observational field notes, I conducted semistructured interviews with 40 clients (approximately 10 women per site) and 14 PSO staff members. Each tape-recorded interview took place in a private setting to ensure confidentiality and lasted between one and two hours. To assure confidentiality and anonymity, I assigned each PSO and person in this study a pseudonym. The client interviews consisted of questions concerning past histories and experiences in sex work, drug use, relationships to family, identity, perceptions of the program, feelings about other clients and staff, reasons for entering the program, future goals, and personal changes. Clients enrolled in each PSO voluntarily or involuntarily, and I interviewed women from both modes of entrée in order to assess its impact on role exiting. My goal was to interview every client at each site, but I was unable to complete this task because I had to work around both program and personal schedules, which made it challenging to secure a block of uninterrupted time to carry out the interviews. Instead, I interviewed a majority of them, while a small minority of PSO clients refused to be interviewed for personal reasons or if they were extremely new to the program and felt unable to comment.

The female street prostitutes in this sample are ethnically and racially diverse, including 22 African Americans, 14 Caucasians, and 4 Hispanics.

Table 1.3 Sample Characteristics of Street Prostitutes (N=40)

		Age	Race/Ethnicity	Time in Prostitution
New Horizons				
	Hayley	32	Hispanic	3
	Derica	49	African American	39
	Marquietta	40	African American	12
	Lily	28	White	15
	Beverly	35	African American	19
	Felicia	40	African American	25
	Patricia	N/A	African American	N/A
	Aretha	42	African American	28
	Ericka	40	African American	10
	Roxanne	51	African American	38
	Susanna	20	White	4
	Amanda	46	Hispanic	6
	Sherita	42	African American	25
Safe Place				
	Veronica	26	African American	10
	Ruthie	32	African American	10
	Jamilah	26	African American	5
	Marleen	35	White	17
	Olivia	28	African American	1
	Stephanie	41	White	27
	Sandra	33	African American	8
	Annie	N/A	White	N/A
	Nancy	33	White	3
	Carla	21	White	8
Phoenix				
	Melissa	42	White	17
	Evie	38	White	15
	Shawnta	45	African American	10
	Rochelle	37	African American	12
	Desiree	20	African American	9
	Hilda	29	African American	5
	Denise	30	African American	1
	Leslie	34	White	20
Seeds				
	Gabriela	31	African American	10
	Cynthia	38	White	16
	Jacqueline	41	African American	25
	Lindsay	43	White	12
	Joyce	24	African American	1
	Maricela	32	Hispanic	16
	Bella	32	Hispanic	1
	Jamie	N/A	White	N/A
	Jessica	N/A	White	N/A

Table 1.3 lists the prostitutes in this study according to PSO, age, race/ethnicity, and longevity in sex work. They ranged in age from 20 to 51, with a mean age of 35 years old. A majority had children (83 percent), and although many were estranged from them, they hoped to reestablish a relationship in the future.

Given the racial and ethnic diversity among prostitutes, their history in sex work, and their general distrust of authority figures, I was particularly conscious of my position as a white, middle-class researcher studying this vulnerable population. Scholars argue that researchers need to be extra sensitive and nonexploitative when studying vulnerable populations, and can do so by allowing interviewees to use their own voices to tell their stories as a way to offset the power imbalance inherent in interviewer–interviewee relationships.[43] As a result, I conducted semistructured interviews that encouraged the women to tell their stories, prompted further by questions rather than curtailing their responses strictly to my interview questions. In response, the interviewees appeared relaxed and talkative, setting the pace and length of the interview. I believe this strategy alleviated some of the alienating effects that interviews can produce among vulnerable subjects. In fact, after the interview ended, many stated that they found it therapeutic.

I also interviewed 14 PSO staff members, approximately a few per site. These interview questions focused on organizational goals, how they were carried out, conflict management, client supervision, perceptions of the PSO, success of the PSO and the clients, and future program goals and plans. Based on this data, I was able to assess the extent to which organizational goals influenced client role exiting, got a sense of program policies and rules, and identify program desired outcomes for clients. Table 1.4 lists the names of central PSO staff members according to their affiliation and position.

Finally, there are limitations to this sample and study. I draw on data from four ethnographic case studies of PSOs with four samples of female street prostitutes. This analysis includes a meaningful cross-section of prostitutes who work in urban contexts and showcases how the exiting process unfolds for those immersed within these specific PSOs. The richness of the data allows for an in-depth examination of the ways organizational settings

Table 1.4 Staff Member by Affiliation

Site	Name	Position
New Horizons	Pamela	Executive Director
	Rayna	Chief Operating Officer
	Thomas	Chief Program Officer
	Ma S.	Residential Director
	Mark	Chief Development Officer
Safe Place	Beth	Program Manager
	Kathy	Counselor and Residential Supervisor
	John	Director of Services
Phoenix	Sally	Residential Director
	Janine	Case Manager
	Paula	Residential Coordinator
Seeds	Marissa	Executive Director
	Melanie	Lead Educator and Facilitator
	Judy	Research and Development Director

influence the social-psychological phases inherent to exiting street-level sex work. I believe this comparative approach strengthens the generalizability of these findings. However, I do not contend that the experiences of those in this study are necessarily representative of all street prostitutes or even to the exiting process across sex workers (and others leaving deviant or criminal roles). Future research can help clarify the generalizability of this study.

Outline of the Book

My intention for this book is to provide a nuanced, comparative analysis of the exiting process for female street prostitutes as they are immersed within prostitute-serving organizations. Each chapter draws on inter-views, conversations, and observations of PSO staff members and clients within these programs to flush out the possible exiting trajectories. I structure the book according to the phases of the career in prostitution:

entrance, experience during, and then the process of role exiting. The last topic is the primary focus of this study, and it unfolds in three stages (each of which comprises a book chapter): initial exit, role distancing, and new role embracement and identity change.

Chapter 2 draws on first-hand accounts of prostitutes located in four US cities in order to assess their entrance pathways into the trade and their experiences on the streets. I present a typology of pathways that are influenced by age of onset (adolescence versus adulthood). As they discussed their experiences, the women noted both positive and negative aspects of sex work. However, their narratives also imply that the longer they worked in street prostitution the more difficult and unmanageable their lives became, and the toll of prostitution mounted. This chapter presents a portrayal of life in street-level sex work for these women that sets the stage for the subsequent phases of role exit.

Chapter 3 examines the first phase of role exiting—*initial exits*—that encompasses how and why women left street sex work and entered a PSO. In this chapter, I identify the factors that resulted in women's enrollment in a PSO, a crucial stage in this transition. I emphasize two internal factors and two external factors that together facilitate this placement. The internal factors consisted of women's individual reasons for exiting (or personal motivations) and turning points that instigate change. The external factors, which are especially integral to initial exits, included women's knowledge of a PSO and the assistance of personal bridges. The accounts from sex workers suggest that this was not a seamless passage, but rather resulted from a complex confluence of events and experiences.

Chapter 4 sheds light on the second phase of role exiting—*role distancing*—where some women exhibit a separation from the role associated with prostitution. They signal these changes to staff and other clients via their talk and behavior. I explore how the organizational cultures of PSOs impact client role distancing. Using field note observations and interviews, I call attention to organizational and socialization practices as they prompt clients to indicate their disengagement from sex work to those around them. I contrast these individuals with recalcitrant clients, who either do not engage in role distancing or express conflict over leaving their role, and offer explanations for their stagnation connected to organizational cultures.

The focus of chapter 5 is on the third phase of role exiting—*role embracement and identity change*—where women demonstrate they have adopted an alternative role and sense of self through their behavior and talk. Similar to the previous phase, organizational attributes and control mechanisms are closely connected to these client alterations. By employing these practices, I conclude that two PSOs (through their members) exerted significant pressure on clients to undergo a role and identity change, while the remaining two did not. As a result, clients who experienced this change were clustered in particular PSOs. I note that additional factors also impact clients' willingness to move into this phase, including commitment-building mechanisms, personal commitment levels to role change, and longevity in the program.

Finally, in chapter 6, I summarize the main findings and highlight the implications of this analysis for understanding exits from prostitution, the process of leaving deviant roles and identities, and the organizational impact on such transitions. I discuss the future trajectories of the women who complete the role-exiting process, and explore the ways they attempt to sustain these new roles and identities as they transition out of PSOs and reintegrate into mainstream society. Although most of the women in this sample are in the midst of role exiting, a handful of them have either completed it or are at the tail end of the process. I present their accounts and experiences in order to reveal the obstacles and challenges that accompany this radical shift in lifestyle. I then address the issue of the permanency of exits as it relates to long-term desistance, and note some of the difficulties involved with this assessment. Finally, I provide structural, legal, and social recommendations that hold potential to improve the quality of life for street-level sex workers, changes that can help address the social problem of prostitution.

2

All in a Day's Work

The Good, Bad, and Ugly

When Derica, an African American, was 10 years old she became a prostitute. Among the women I spoke with this was the youngest age of initial involvement in the sex trade. When I inquired about why she first engaged in prostitution, she prefaced her explanation by admitting that male family members had molested her for years. She recalled, "To be honest and truthful I didn't realize I got involved in prostitution at such a very young age until recently. After some reflection and counseling it became clearer . . . my uncle that used to touch me he always gave me candy or pennies or something afterwards. That was the beginning of it but I just didn't realize it at that time." She learned from these early experiences that she could get rewards for sex acts, and performed them from that point forward. It was not long before she entered street-level prostitution—a decision she claimed was fueled by her attraction to the lifestyle, which she believed was full of glamour, money, and material possessions. This confluence of personal circumstances and pervasive cultural norms led her to the pathway of prostitution.

In contrast, Shawnta, African American, first performed street-level prostitution when she was thirty-five. Her motivation stemmed solely from an intense desire to acquire drugs. The prospect of selling sex emerged after a few men propositioned her after they got high together. It became even more appealing after her previous sources of income— government-issued checks and money from boyfriends—could no longer sustain her growing drug habit. She provided insight into her thinking at that time: "I thought, hey, I could go out there and be assertive and get it [money] myself." After a few successful encounters, she recognized her ability to quickly earn large amounts of money for sex, and it became her primary method to finance her drug of choice: crack cocaine.

The individual motivations and pathways into sex work varied greatly between Derica and Shawnta. They illustrate a few of the types of entrance pathways based upon age of onset: one was an adolescent and the other an adult. The question of why women enter prostitution is an age-old one that seems to repeatedly surface among researchers, community and state agencies, and concerned citizens. By relying on in-depth interviews with four samples of street prostitutes, I explore pathways into the trade by age of entry, which influences tenure in street-level sex work.

The previous chapter provides an overview of the theoretical explanations for leaving prostitution, deviance, and crime. However, in order to fully understand the exiting process—the tail end of their sex work career—it is important to first examine the beginning and middle portions of these careers as well. The young age of those who first entered prostitution as minors may immediately serve as a red flag warning for some readers, implying that sex trafficking and coercion facilitated their engagement. This stance coincides with the belief that many females and adolescents do not voluntarily choose sex work, but rather are forced into the trade due to circumstances and predatory adults. A growing worldwide antitrafficking movement draws attention to this phenomenon and ultimately works to protect those impacted by it. When it is against one's will, most would agree that the performance of sex acts can cause great harm and trauma for that individual.

There are a number of recent academic studies that highlight the widespread nature of sex trafficking, reveal the exploitation of children and young women, and call attention to the criminal elements and networks that perpetuate it.[1] Certain scholars argue that no adolescents can voluntarily engage in prostitution because of their age and vulnerability; therefore, they are coerced into the trade.[2] Others have called these widely held assumptions into question. In particular, they draw attention to a variety of concerns with much of the sex trafficking research. Some question whether the number of trafficked individuals is exaggerated, if case studies are overgeneralized, the degree to which empirical results suffer from sample selection bias, or if conclusions have adequate empirical support.[3] A handful of studies even highlight the agency of trafficked persons, both adolescents and adults, which belie a majority of published work on this topic.[4] For instance, criminologists Ko-Lin Chin and James Finckenauer report that none of the women in their study claim to be "subjected to abduction, force or coercion in the process of entering the commercial sex business overseas."[5]

I recognize the importance of having these debates, especially when it comes to children and those forced to perform sex work against their will. Below I analyze the age of initial entrance of individuals into prostitution, and separate the samples into adolescent and adult onset. I do not repudiate the claim that some of the youngsters were coerced or lured into sex work by predatory adults, yet I rely on their narratives to illuminate the conditions surrounding their entrance and accordingly devise pathway types. My data may also incite long-standing feminist and academic disagreements about the nature of sex work itself and whether those involved actually have a choice regarding this decision.[6] This book cannot satisfactorily address the issues surrounding trafficking or even articulate a compelling stance in the voluntary or involuntary debate, because the qualitative data either present contradictory evidence or are not sufficient to make a case. Additionally, while these topics are salient and certainly warrant further exploration, the purpose of this book is to primarily illuminate the transition out of the trade.

I find that entrance into prostitution constitutes four pathways aligned according to age categories of adolescence or adulthood. After identifying the pathways, I assess the range of experiences women had while working on the streets, both positive and negative, and how their perceptions of the work shifted the longer they remained in it.[7]

Explanations for Female Entrance into Prostitution

The women in this study provided detailed accounts of why and how they first began to work in prostitution. Many of these explanations support the findings of previous work on this topic, including sexual abuse, running away, socialization and cultural influences, interpersonal networks, financial necessity, drug addiction, and psychological characteristics.[8] The susceptibility model suggests that it is the combination of psychological characteristics (i.e., alienation and feelings of worthlessness) and tragic events (such as sexual assault) that make particular women more likely to engage in prostitution.[9] Accordingly, when certain personality attributes are coupled with personal crisis, females become more susceptible to engage in sex work. Derica's circumstances and perceptions as a child could lend support to this model.

Personal social networks and exposure to prostitution can also be a root cause of entry, which encompasses both interpersonal contacts with and encouragement from others who are involved in the subculture of sex work.[10] Such an argument is reminiscent of the cultural deviance theoretical perspective, which attributes crime to a set of values, attitudes, and ideas that are reinforced by peers and associates.[11] The acquisition of these norms becomes more likely when one's personal networks consist of individuals who uphold and perpetuate them. This theory, as it applies to prostitution, has some empirical support. Researchers Jody Raphael and Deborah Shapiro, who conducted a study on Chicago-based female street prostitutes, found one-third of their sample had a household member work in prostitution where they grew up, and more than two-thirds reported they were encouraged by another individual to work as a prostitute to earn money.[12]

Cultural deviance is not simply about interpersonal exchanges bolstered by values and attitudes, but is also significantly influenced by structural conditions, such as class. In fact, economic necessity is the prominent explanation for entrance into sex work. This is especially relevant among disadvantaged women, immersed within similar communities, who turn to prostitution as a survival strategy. Evidence indicates that when women lack viable legal alternatives, they, along with many of their community associates, are more likely to perceive prostitution as a feasible option for income.[13] It follows then that those who enter sex work due to limited economic opportunities may perceive it as a rational decision.[14]

Another culturally related phenomenon among sex workers is the pervasiveness of drug use and addiction. This trend is well documented in numerous studies on street prostitutes, and the money to secure drug acquisition can serve as the impetus to enter into the trade.[15] For certain drug-addicted women, Shawnta being one of them, prostitution may be the most accessible and viable way to finance their habit, especially among those who lack education and job skills.[16] The causal relationship between drug use and the decision to engage in sex work is not always clear-cut; some women use drugs only recreationally prior to engaging in prostitution, but their habit intensifies over time when it becomes a coping mechanism.[17] Ultimately, once the two become interdependent, it creates conditions that embroil individuals in the trade.

Although numerous theories attempt to illuminate pathways into street-level sex work, there is sparse nuanced examination of how these pathways are tied to and shaped by an individual's age of entry.[18] This is noteworthy given that the criminological life-course development approach stresses that age of offending is particularly important for

Table 2.1 Typology of Pathways into Prostitution

Type of Entrance	Characteristics	Sample Size
18 AND UNDER		
Fleeing Abuse & Reclaiming Control	Childhood physical/sexual abuse, runaway behavior, perception of sex work as empowering, some use of pimps	8
Normal	Economic motivation, learned from family and friends, viewed sex work as exciting and glamorous	6
19 AND UP		
Sustain Drug Addiction	Family history of drug use, drug addicted, morally conflicted about sex work	10
Survival	Means of survival, homeless, fueled by tragic circumstances or events	6
Other	Do not fit into other categories	3

establishing trajectories of criminal activity.[19] In order to identify pathways into prostitution as they may be influenced by age of onset, as well as the implications of this coupling, I had to separate my sample according to their entrance age. The two age categories consisted of adolescent entry (18 years or less) and adult entry (19 years and older). I then coded for entrance pathways and found patterns that varied based upon age categories (see Table 2.1).[20] Those who entered prostitution during adolescence cited two pathways: *prostitution to reclaim control of one's sexuality* and *prostitution as normal.* In comparison, women who initially entered as adults noted two different pathways: *prostitution to sustain drug addiction* and *prostitution for survival.* The final category of *others* contains a few females who demonstrated some combination of pathways, and therefore did not fit neatly into the other four types.[21] While no pattern is seamless and there is some overlap across types, overall the typology encompasses a range of motivations and pathways into prostitution that varies according to age.

Adolescent Female Motivations for Entering Prostitution
Fleeing Abuse and Reclaiming Control

One common theme among those who entered sex work as adolescents was they came from families with high levels of dysfunction, including substance-addicted parents, absent parents, or exposure to sexually, physically, and emotionally abusive adults. As a result, these individuals felt they had little control over their own lives and decided to escape their home situations in order to take care of themselves. A majority of those (57 percent) who entered prostitution as adolescents discussed their entry as an attempt to regain control over their lives and their sexuality. In short, they framed this decision as their reaction to some form of childhood victimization—sexual molestation, rape, incest, or physical assault. Over time, the abuse became so unbearable for these girls they opted to run away, flee their families, and fend for themselves on the streets. One way to do that was to engage in street prostitution as a means of financial support.

One African American woman, Veronica, stated that she entered prostitution at 16 due to the ongoing molestation she experienced in her family of origin: "I left home at an early age because there was some molestation in my family. I went into prostitution for money and to rebel from my parents." Similarly, Desiree linked her reason for engaging in prostitution at the age of 11 to early sexual abuse that occurred within the confines of her grandmother's house, who was her guardian. She recalled:

> My grandmother was also engaged in a lot of activities such as selling drugs, doing drugs, renting out the rooms of her house and stuff like that. So staying was basically out of the question . . . because she had so many men in the house and I had been sexually molested and raped a lot of times by them. I didn't want to stay there anymore and put up with that. I was out of there.

The ongoing abuse typically generated feelings of disempowerment for these young girls, particularly when the abuse took place within their household and at the hands of family members. Thus, their accounts often underscore their desire to find a way to reclaim control over their sexuality, heightened after leaving that tainted setting. In an effort to repudiate their sense of powerlessness, some chose to wield their sexuality to garner control over men and also earn a profit by exchanging sex for money. Felicia, an African American, summed up this sentiment in her account: "At the time it [prostitution] gave me a sense of control because I had been molested as a child. So it was like at some point it felt like I was getting a revenge for the predators in my life at that time." Stephanie, Caucasian, provided a similar justification when she described how she initially entered prostitution: "Because from my childhood, I had been molested. And then as time went on, I was still getting molested, so I got tired. And I said, 'Well, if a man going to take it from me, why not sell myself? I get to make the choice then.'"

For certain adolescents, a male figure facilitated their entrance into sex work after they left their home of origin. Many researchers would now consider these instances as cases of sex trafficking. The girls perceived these males as boyfriends, although they also acted as their pimps. Past empirical studies argue that there is a general decline of street prostitutes' reliance on pimps, yet that may not be the case for adolescents.[22] Only a few individuals in this sample stated that a pimp initially pulled them into the trade. Aretha was an African American teenage runaway who fled her home due to an abusive father. Once on the streets, she met an older man who took a liking to her. He started out as her boyfriend and then transitioned to the role of pimp as he arranged her sexual encounters with customers. She explained this shift as gradual:

> I used to run away from home a lot because my father used to beat us. So I ran away from home and I met this guy and he told me—I explained to him how my father beated on us—he said, "Well I'm not gonna beat you. And you can call me Daddy." He used to buy me anything I wanted, whatever, no matter how much it was. He treated me nice and liked me.

Before long, Aretha discovered that these gifts had to be earned. She clarified, "Later on in the relationship he said, 'Now you gotta go do this [acts of prostitution] in order to keep me buying you those things.' So I did it." Aretha was enticed as an adolescent to engage in sex work because she perceived that these acts pleased her boyfriend-pimp and sustained her acquisition of material goods.

Leslie, who is white, recalled that she engaged in prostitution at approximately 14 because her boyfriend introduced her to the idea and encouraged her to do so. After she agreed, he became her pimp and garnered much of her money:

> He said, "Well if you like me, would you like to make some money?" So I'm like, "Well yeah, okay." So he took me over to different men's houses, he said, "You do whatever they want you to do . . . They'll give you money

and when you get the money you bring it back and give it to me." And that's that I did, not knowing that I was prostituting because again I was young and didn't know.

It is clear that at the onset of prostitution, certain adolescent girls perceived sex work as a way to reclaim some control over their sexuality—they could partake in sexual encounters and earn money. However, as I illustrate later in this chapter, their perceptions changed over time as the difficulties of the work mounted. Ironically, despite their initial impressions, the girls who entered prostitution at the prodding of a male figure quickly relinquished much of their autonomy and earnings to him within a short time, in effect negating all sense of control over their own sexuality. With this type of arrangement, working in street prostitution under a pimp is often far from empowering.[23]

Working in Prostitution Is Normal

The other pathway into prostitution among adolescent females consisted of the normalization of sex work. Among this group, approximately 43 percent fell within this category and described prostitution as a commonplace activity in their surrounding neighborhoods. As a result, these individuals viewed prostitution (and sex work) as a viable option for income. Beverly, African American, was exposed to prostitution through family members, as her father was a pimp and routinely kept company with prostitutes. She explained how these activities were a memorable aspect of her childhood and adolescence:

> I wanted to be with my dad and of course these things were going on in my dad's household . . . because I told you my dad was a dope dealer and pimp, so that's when I became attracted to the lifestyle. The glamour part of it, you know, I saw the dressing up and the makeup and really that was the attraction for me. Not really knowing at that time all that entails. You know my dad kept a lot of street people around and that's how I met this

guy that eventually introduced me to prostitution. He basically became my pimp. I was doing it regularly by sixteen.

Beverly's entry into prostitution was fueled through routine socialization with individuals affiliated with the sex trade, including her father. Therefore, it is not surprising that she learned values, beliefs, and behaviors that corresponded with this subculture lifestyle, all of which ultimately facilitated her pathway into sex work.

Another common theme, alluded to by Beverly, was the perception that working in prostitution was glamorous and exciting. As these adolescent girls observed women working in the trade, they often regarded the work and the accoutrements as sophisticated. Thus, they came to believe that prostitution was a way to achieve status and validation in an environment where few other models for upward mobility existed. Jacqueline, an African American, surmised: "After my father died we were so poor and in that area that's all you see are prostitutes and pimps. The girls are wearing nice clothes and making money, that's what I wanted too, so that's how it started for me." Although she had also been molested as a young girl, Derica did not run away from home to flee abuse. Instead she cited cultural explanations that fueled her performance of street-level prostitution as an adolescent:

> [I did it] because of the money, the excitement, my environment. When I grew up in the late 60s, the movies and people were glamorizing pimps and hustlers and stuff . . . All I seen was the money, the furs, the jewelry and the talk . . . so I wanted that for myself. I started and I got a rush out of that quick money, that fast living.

For both of these adolescent pathways, cultural deviance theory is particularly relevant. In both trajectories, the decision to engage in prostitution was facilitated by social networks and interpersonal relationships with adults and informed by the surrounding cultural norms, values, and attitudes that tolerated (or even promoted) sex work as a viable means through which to acquire goods and status.

Motivations for Entering Prostitution as Adults
Sustaining the Drug Habit

In contrast to the pathways of adolescents into prostitution, the women who entered as adults offered alternative explanations. A little over half of those (53 percent) who first engaged in prostitution as adults attributed their entrance to drug addiction. Most of these women were immersed within environments where drug use was prevalent and they routinely interacted with other drug users. Shawnta, for instance, first started working as a prostitute at the age of thirty-five. When asked what prompted her to do so, she unequivocally stated:

> Because of my drug addiction. I found out that would enable me to get money for drugs—quicker than waiting on county checks or a boyfriend to bring it to me. I could go out there and be assertive and get it myself. When I was around men when we were getting loaded, I noticed that their behavior would change once they started smoking [crack]. And I was propositioned once or twice but then it occurred to me one day—hey, I could sell my body and get some money. I tried it and it worked.

When posed with the same question, Denise, who is African American, responded, "I have an addiction to money and drugs. Plain and simple." And Joyce concurred, "Once I started [crack] and got hooked is when I first entered prostitution to support my growing habit." For these women, sex work served as a way to support their existing—and considerable—substance addiction.

Compared to the adolescent onset group, where cultural deviance, prior abuse, or familial relationships shaped their perceptions and lead them to perform sex acts, an interesting moral contradiction existed among the women who entered via this pathway. Ericka, an African American, recalled:

I used to see other girls out there and I'm like "How could they do that?" Then I had such a strong need for a drug ... it [prostitution] wasn't something that I liked to do actually, you know, but the need for the drug was so great that it took priority. Nothing else mattered. I was willing to go out there and sell my body.

And Cynthia, who is white, explained how she initially struggled with moral beliefs about engaging in prostitution at the age of 22:

It was for the money to support my substance abuse—crack. When I first started prostituting it had a very big impact on me. I would only work when it was dark out. I knew it was wrong. I didn't want my children or family members to see me. God forbid if someone should see me . . . I was so ashamed. As the progression of my disease picked up sooner or later it was early hours of the morning, then it was afternoon, then it was 24 hours a day. Then it became seven days a week. The progression of my disease took hold. And nothing matters. You use to live and live to use.

They espoused strong moral condemnation of prostitution, but still engaged in it due to their relentless desire for drugs. In fact, they asserted that their addiction to drugs made them more amenable to the trade by rendering their long-standing mores and values about the work less salient. And as their addictions progressed they violated their previously held judgments about prostitution, as it became a viable means to earn quick cash for drugs. For the women discussed above, severe drug use pulled them into sex work and kept them in the trade for the duration of their addiction, a phenomenon also confirmed in past research.[24]

Survival Sex

Among adult onset prostitutes, approximately 32 percent described their entry into prostitution as a means of survival because it provided a way to earn money to eat and pay rent for housing. For example, Bella, Hispanic, explained, "I lived in the streets and there was no other way to maintain myself for food, clothes . . . it was really hard for me." To survive, Bella sold drugs but resorted to prostitution "when the sales weren't coming through." Before long it became a routine practice for her. And recall Marquietta's explanation for engaging in prostitution as an adult:

> I was still married to my second husband. We were separated. He left me in Atlanta stranded. He packed up our things, my kids, and left while— during a time when I was in a mental hospital. I had a real bad breakdown. And when I got out I told him that I couldn't live with him for a minute, that I needed time to adjust. So I moved in with a girlfriend of mine, and during the time I was at her house he packed up everything and moved back North and left me in Atlanta stranded. I guess he felt that my relatives were here so I would be okay . . . but it kind of messed me up. I ended up prostituting my way back to the Midwest because I had no money, nothing to my name. I had no other options.

Amanda, a Hispanic who began selling sex for money at 40, recalled it was due to her being homeless after a confluence of tragic events that included her divorce, her daughter's incarceration, and her grandson's placement under state guardianship after she was no longer deemed suitable to care for him. She became severely depressed and left her house and job to live on the streets, where she began dabbling in street prostitution to survive:

> I became homeless before I started prostitution. And I started hanging out with girls that were doing it and I got into it. Nobody forced me into it. I never had a pimp. I worked for me. While homeless, I also started the addiction of crack. From the addiction of crack, I needed to keep in prostitution because I had to find a way to make money to support my habit and still keep my cell phone and pay for rent if I stayed anywhere overnight.

In contrast to those who resorted to prostitution because they were economically motivated to sustain their drug addiction, these women turned to sex work for survival. They may have also regularly used drugs, but their primary explanation revolved around acquiring money for basic life necessities (e.g., securing food and shelter, paying bills). Amanda's case suggests that she initially performed sex work because she was homeless. However, it is also evident in her statement that her drug addiction was escalating over time and the cycle of remaining in prostitution for drugs was soon to commence. Those subsumed within this category are unique because when they first engaged in prostitution they were not addicted to drugs, although within a relatively short time period this changed. These accounts indicate that poverty and lack of resources can serve as a catalyst to pull women into sex work, as it is one of the most readily available opportunities for making money among disadvantaged people.[25]

A Range of Feelings

Many of the events and circumstances prompting entrance into prostitution are undesirable, and even traumatic, for this group of sex workers. Yet to assign a monolithic experience to them is misleading, as these accounts indicate that their perceptions and assessments of sex work are complex, multifaceted, and temporal. Feelings of glamour, prestige, self-sufficiency, and self-esteem are embedded within some of the explanations presented by those who engaged in prostitution when adolescents. Even among the adult onset group, there were acknowledgments of the positive aspects of the work itself. After a period when she first entertained the prospect of sex work by walking the streets with a fellow prostitute, Evie, Caucasian, highlighted some benefits of it in her recollections: "It was kind of exciting . . . And I got a thrill out of the guys whistling at me with my miniskirt on and all." Although African American Rochelle originally engaged in prostitution because she was unemployed, when asked if there were other reasons that shaped her decision she admitted, "I was in my late twenties and I had just had my second child. And honestly, I also thought it was exciting."

Beyond the excitement and attention some prostitutes experienced, a few women internalized the male attention and stated that it elevated their self-esteem. While these claims were not common, they suggest that prostitutes experience a range of feelings and emotions that fluctuate and are even contradictory. Shawnta, who was known as DoubleDee on the streets (a reference to her large breast size), drew connections between the male attention and her increased self-worth. She elaborated: "When I was on the streets the men would be catcalling, whistling, hitting corners, honking. It was exciting. But that was the object—to attract, to entice. [When I did that] then I felt good about myself." Lily, who is white, similarly reflected: "I guess it made me feel good because guys paid attention to me. You know, being a prostitute, I was just [gasp] 'look at all these guys stopping for me.' It made me feel so good." Melissa's response poignantly captures the complexity of feelings she experienced in response to intense male scrutiny:

> Because believe it or not, when you are actually out on the streets it's flattering. But most of the time it's tearing down your self-esteem, but at the same time you think you have all this esteem built up in you. I used to think, oh gosh, you know, these guys all want me. And it becomes a very flattering situation. It's a whole different lifestyle. Sometimes you feel like a celebrity when you are out there.

Feelings of empowerment, attractiveness, glamour, and excitement emerged as positive outcomes of working in prostitution for certain women. However, these feelings were not sustained for long durations after the initial entrance period. In fact, the longer individuals remained in prostitution the number and salience of negative experiences associated with sex work seemed to grow, and ultimately colored their perceptions of the trade.

I find that pathways into prostitution clustered according to age of onset are linked to overall time spent working on the streets, a phenomenon that appears to exact a greater toll on prostitutes. To assess length of time in the trade, I list the age of entrance and initial exit via PSOs to

provide estimates of time in prostitution (see Table 2.2).[26] It is interesting to note that those who entered as adolescents remained in the trade
for significantly longer periods of time (a mean of 21 years) compared to
those who began as adults (a mean of eight years).[27] What does the term
"toll" encompass? I delve into the meaning of this concept derived from
the narratives of the women in this study.

Table 2.2 Age of Entry, Exit, and Time in the Trade

		Age of entrance	Age of exit	Time in (years)
Adolescent entry	LILY	13	28	15
N=14	BEVERLY	16	35	19
	FELICIA	15	40	25
	ARETHA	14	42	28
	ROXANNE	13	51	38
	SUSANNA	16	20	4
	MARICELA	16	32	16
	JACQUELINE	16	41	25
	DERICA	10	49	39
	VERONICA	16	26	10
	MARLEEN	18	35	17
	STEPHANIE	14	41	27
	DESIREE	11	20	9
	LESLIE	14	34	20
	Average time in trade			20.86
Adult entry	CYNTHIA	22	38	16
N=19	LINDSAY	31	43	12
	JOYCE	24	25	1
	BELLA	31	32	1
	GABRIELA	21	31	10
	AMANDA	40	46	6
	ERICKA	30	40	10
	MARQUIETTA	28	40	12
	HAYLEY	29	32	3
	JAMILAH	21	26	5
	OLIVIA	27	28	1
	SANDRA	25	33	8
	RUTHIE	22	32	10
	MELISSA	25	42	17
	EVIE	23	38	15
	SHAWNTA	35	45	10
	ROCHELLE	25	37	12
	HILDA	24	29	5
	DENISE	29	30	1
	Average time in trade			8.16

The Toll of Prostitution

While age of onset is linked to particular pathways into the trade, this marker also suggests other implications for street prostitutes. The visible and illegal nature of street prostitution produces many hardships for those who engage in this form of sex work, including high levels of stigmatization, criminalization, and violence. I find that those who begin prostitution as adolescents tend to remain in prostitution for extended durations, a phenomenon that often amplifies the toll they experience. Sociologist Bernadette Barton notes the toll that exists among exotic dancers and defines it in the following manner: "[The toll is] a complex accumulation of experiences in strip bars and societal stigma both within and without them that tax the energy and self-esteem of late-career dancers."[28] Although both populations fall under the umbrella of "sex worker," the signs of a toll among street prostitutes varies considerably from that of strippers. The rich, qualitative accounts from these female street prostitutes indicate that the toll for them consists of the following: the accumulation of violent encounters, elevated levels of exhaustion, heightened stigma and broken relationships with family members, increased drug addiction as a way to cope with the difficulties of the work, and multiple arrests and jail sentences.

The first indicator of the toll is the amount and intensity of violent interactions that ensues for street prostitutes. An abundance of research underscores the pervasiveness of violence within urban environments. A few notable studies emphasize that minority groups, who are immersed within poor neighborhoods, tend to be particularly susceptible.[29] Similarly, empirical research reveals that female street prostitutes, many of whom are poor women of color, experience the greatest rates and risk of abuse and assault vis-à-vis all other sex workers.[30] Even though violence and assault can occur at any time throughout one's career in prostitution, it was the women who remained in the trade for long durations who drew attention to the significant impact violence had on them. Marleen, white, who had engaged in prostitution at the age of 18 and remained in the trade for 17 years, listed a litany of past violent encounters related to the work: "I've been raped, woken up rolled up in a tarp, left for dead, had my lung collapse in a street fight, and more. It's amazing I'm still alive." Stephanie, who was 14 years old when she first started and worked as a prostitute for 27 years, also emphasized the violence and abuse she endured when she described what her life was like as a sex worker: "I was raped many times and left for dead, having people cut my face up, and my eye was permanently damaged. I was almost killed by my last john and I ran for my life." The reality is that those who remain in street-level sex work for substantial periods of time have greater exposure to violence and assault by customers, pimps, or others within the street subculture, making this a central concern for late-career prostitutes.

Feelings of exhaustion also suggest a toll associated with street prostitution, as those who remain in prostitution for many years cite fatigue as a prominent outcome of their work. Lily, 28 years old, who worked as a prostitute for 15 years, claimed these feelings were so significant they made her consider exiting the lifestyle altogether. She explained: "I was tired of prostituting and wanted to try and change my life so I could do something else because I'm getting way too old for it. By the end, I was so tired I just sat on the sidewalk from sheer exhaustion until the cops found me." Roxanne, a 51-year-old African American woman, who initially engaged in prostitution at age 13, also admitted that she was seriously affected by exhaustion stemming from the sex trade: "I realized that I wanted to stop this lifestyle because I'm way too old for this shit . . . I just got tired. I'm a mother of 11 kids and 15 grandkids. At this point in my life I shouldn't be doing that." When probed to describe specifically the ways in which she felt tired, Roxanne referenced both mental and physical exhaustion: "I was so tired and ill that I went to the hospital, I barely made it to the hospital. Around that time I also got depressed, that's another issue I struggled with—depression."

Another feature of the toll of this work is when women are stigmatized and labeled by their loved ones, which has deleterious effects on the quality of these relationships. Several women spoke of the stigma they experienced as a result of prostitution and their subsequent feelings of shame that emerged. As these factors compounded, their familial relationships were subjected to additional strain. Marquietta worked in prostitute for

12 years and described how the shame she felt over her actions caused her to sever ties with her family members: "Once my family found out I was in county jail on prostitution charges, well . . . I didn't see them for years after that because I was embarrassed and ashamed of what they would think about me and my lifestyle. I didn't try to get in touch and neither did they." Felicia, who entered prostitution at 15 and remained in the trade for 25 years, recalled how her relationships with family members completely deteriorated when her brother saw her flagging down customers on the streets. The subsequent interaction between them culminated in a physical altercation, which she summed up in the following way: "[He] got so angry with me that he physically assaulted me." The stigma and shame the women experienced as a result of their participation in sex work drastically colored their perceptions of it, especially when it resulted in alienation from family members and an overall breakdown of social support.

Extensive drug use and addiction is another indicator of the toll derived from prostitution. Some women initially entered prostitution to sustain deeply entrenched drug habits; however, they also claimed that their addictions grew worse the longer they remained in the trade. Among those who did not routinely use drugs when they began sex work, many soon relied on them to cope with the difficulties of the work. Melissa, a prostitute for 17 years, admitted that she occasionally used drugs prior to working in the sex trade, and her habit grew worse after her entrance. She admitted the quick influx of money and the lifestyle associated with the work eradicated most of her previous responsibilities: "When I started working the street it got even worse because I didn't have commitments to make. As I got more money I could just blow it on drugs."

Derica, who entered prostitution at age 10 and spent a total of 39 years in the trade, discussed how drugs became the way she coped with shame and stigma: "Yes, it bothered me that my family found out what I was doing and what they thought about me, but I just went and got high so I wouldn't have to have to deal with it." Recall that Cynthia felt considerable shame and stigma about engaging in prostitution. She admitted that heroin helped assuage those feelings, which she desperately wanted to avoid. By the time she was arrested, her long-term heroin addiction rendered her physically and mentally incapacitated:

> When I was arrested I was so sick and so sick and tired that they had to arraign me from the doorway. My drug of choice was heroin. I couldn't even walk to stand in front of the judge so they arraigned me from the doorway, that's how sick I was.

Girls and women provide disparate reasons for entering prostitution, yet when they remain in the trade for long periods of time, drug addiction is inevitably a key factor that sustains their participation. The above accounts suggest that drug use was a coping strategy to manage feelings of fear, shame, worthlessness, and powerlessness. Yet it also granted a brief emotional and psychological respite from the negative experiences and tragedies that had transpired in many of their lives.

The final indicator of a toll is the establishment of criminal records due to prostitution and corresponding drug use or possession. Each time a woman was arrested for prostitution or drug charges, she received stiffer punitive sentences and her criminal history grew more substantial. Due to their visibility, most women were arrested at some point in their careers; however, those who remained in sex work for long durations were more likely to accrue criminal sentences and serve time in jail or prison. Desiree had a substantial history of arrests and jail time accumulated during her nine years of prostitution. She was "burned out" and felt that the costs of the trade were becoming too great as she faced another long stint in jail: "I was on parole and I got busted for prostitution again. I knew I was going back to prison for a long time. At that point, I knew something had to change."

Aretha, who engaged in prostitution for 28 years, also expressed that returning to prison was her biggest fear and caused her substantial worry. She espoused: "I had been to the penitentiary twice, one more arrest and I would have gone away for a long, long time. I became so scared of getting in a car with an undercover cop . . . that was a big fear for me.

Because when you go to prison, you don't really know if you'll get out alive." It follows that those who experienced multiple interactions with the criminal justice system had heightened anxiety about subsequent arrests and incarceration, given that these punitive measures became stiffer each time. The palpable fear, worry, and emotional stress constituted a major psychological toll for these women.

Implications of Entrance Pathways

This chapter illustrates that pathways into sex work align with age of onset (adolescence or adulthood), a connection that has been rarely examined in empirical studies.[31] Adolescent pathways included girls running away from abusive households in an attempt to reclaim control over their sexuality, and girls who considered prostitution a viable way to acquire status and money due to prevalent cultural norms in their surrounding communities. In contrast, adult entrance into prostitution consisted of different pathways. They were propelled into the trade by either intense drug addiction, a phenomenon not yet salient among the adolescent population, or due to survival sex work. The notion of survival sex work dovetails with the feminization of poverty theory, which states that women are driven to commit economic crimes primarily because of their low socioeconomic status.[32] As previously noted, 93 percent of the women in this sample identified as poor and came from lower-class familial backgrounds.

I identify the conditions and risk factors that ultimately become catalysts for female engagement in street-level prostitution and note entrance pathways hold implications for longevity in the trade, which potentially exacerbates the toll experienced by prostitutes. By doing so, I extend prior theoretical analyses on this topic. But such conclusions can also inform policies (both public and criminal) concerned with the prevention of prostitution and their victimization. My findings underscore the need for additional support services that address these issues as they occur among disadvantaged women and girls *prior* to their entrance. Indeed, mitigating risks for susceptible adolescent girls may be an even greater concern, as my study suggests they are the ones who tend to have longer tenures in sex work and experience the greatest toll.

Additional services could include the nationwide expansion of drug treatment facilities, infusions of monetary aid to disenfranchised neighborhoods to encourage upward mobility, and more effective state intervention in abusive households. They can also take the form of aggressive public campaigns designed to prevent drug use or those intended to dismantle community norms that frame street prostitution as a viable option of work. When preventive measures do not generate the desired results, there should be abundant social services available to help those who are performing sex work and want to leave. The PSOs I examine in this book comprise a network of support services; however, they are unable to supply resources for a majority of those in need without additional—and substantial—financial backing from governmental or private sources. In a related issue, there are too few of these programs nationwide due to limited funding, a fact that restricts their ability to impact the phenomenon of street prostitution on a broad scale.

Recently there has been substantial cultural attention directed toward the plight of underage females in the sex trade. Over time, the criminal justice system and the public has started to adopt a more sympathetic view of adolescents engaged in prostitution, noting their susceptibility and vulnerability. This trend is largely fueled by national and international antisex trafficking campaigns that emphasize the victimization and age of the youth involved. An illustration of this point is found in the terminology related to child prostitution—now often referred to as the Commercial Sexual Exploitation of Children (CSEC)—which is commonly conflated with sex trafficking.[33] The 2007 documentary, *Very Young Girls*, encapsulates this stance and aims to elicit compassion for girls involved in sex work while simultaneously castigating the adults who profit off their efforts.

Various feminist social movements, human rights organizations, and PSOs buttress these efforts as they advocate for legal reform on behalf of minors engaged in prostitution.[34] For example, Girls Educational and

Mentoring Services (GEMS), a 14-year-old PSO, played a key role in getting the Safe Harbor Act passed in New York State in 2008. This state law mandates that adolescent prostitutes be treated as victims and be channeled into services and programs instead of being charged with a crime, and institutes a multiagency program that facilitates their transition out of sex work and reintegration into the community.

The collective advocacy efforts have generated some success, as the US government and criminal justice system have started to implement legal and practical changes, including the Safe Harbor Act, that focus less on punitive measures and more on rehabilitation for minors in street-level prostitution. Women's studies scholar Erin Dubyak describes how the Clinton and Bush administrations have supported antitrafficking efforts (measures often directed toward youth) by passing laws that enact stricter sentences against those who orchestrate it and protect individuals affected by it.[35] Perhaps one of the best-known examples of federal legislation with this agenda is found in the Trafficking Victims Protection Act (TVPA). Dubyak also notes the substantial sums of federal money earmarked to fund groups dedicated to combat trafficking.

Despite this support and these advancements, there is still substantial variation across states regarding the criminal justice system's treatment of underage prostitutes. The few federal laws that have been passed are difficult to uniformly uphold and enforce. As a result, the de facto practices of many state and local level officials, not to mention public opinion, continue to sustain the criminalization of both adolescent and adult prostitutes. On the bright side, the recent, albeit haphazard, changes in US laws and treatment options for minors who perform sex work hold potential to profoundly alter their future trajectories. If they are diverted from the trade at an early age via sanctioned treatment rather than criminalized, and they are able to avoid criminal records or incarceration altogether as a result, the toll of prostitution may be minimized for them.

Unfortunately, the relatively new criminal justice practices implemented by legislation, as well as the shift in public sentiment toward underage prostitutes, have not affected the women included in this study because most are middle-aged adults who have incurred substantial criminalization over the course of their tenure in sex work. They are still deemed criminals and deviants by both the criminal justice system and society. Those who did engage in adolescent prostitution in the past did so at a time when the age of a prostitute had little relevance to how she was publicly labeled, her treatment, or her criminalization.

Throughout this chapter, I argue that age of onset influences pathways into prostitution, which in turn can generate a toll for those who remain in the trade for long durations of time. Even though a few women note some positive benefits of the trade, they are typically apparent early on in their career, and the negative aspects that comprise a toll become increasingly salient over time.[36] While age of entrance does not affect the overall exiting process, the toll experienced by prostitutes can help prompt an initial exit into a PSO (phase one of the overall exiting process). In the next chapter, I explore how indicators of a toll can also serve as personal motivations for leaving sex work altogether.

3

Getting In

From the Streets to the Program

Roxanne engaged in prostitution for 38 years, holding one of the longest tenures of all the women included in this book. She was a known jokester at New Horizons, brandishing a smile just before she began teasing a staff member or fellow resident. Yet during one-on-one conversations when she spoke of more serious matters, her eyes would often fill with tears and her words would dry up mid-sentence as she became lost in thought. She had a very long history of drug addiction, commencing in her teens. Her single mother was a police officer, and often absent from the home; however, this did not deter Roxanne from illicit activities.

Her first foray into sex work was as a stripper, where she lied about her age to get the job. While there she met her "sugar daddy," an older man who gave her money to have sex with him on a regular basis outside of the club. This was her first act of prostitution. When I sat down with her in a quiet room at New Horizons for our interview, her mood was somber. I inquired about her decision to stop and how she entered this program. Roxanne admitted she had never really considered leaving until she became very sick and was hospitalized after a long and intensive drug binge smoking cocaine. A few of her sober friends recommended a detox center, but before she was admitted she went to a county hospital because she felt so ill. While there her mother came to visit her, an emotional interaction that escalated her motivation to quit. After a couple of days in the hospital when her condition stabilized, Roxanne was convinced she would die if she did not get sober, which also meant a cessation of prostitution. The following excerpt is her recollection of the conversation with her mother prior to entering the detox program, the day of her discharge from the hospital:

> I told her, "They [staff from the detox program] gonna pick me up at your house about six or seven o'clock this evening." She said, "Good." I got out and she took me shopping and everything, she bought me some clothes, and then I left to the detox. My mother said, "Goodbye." I said, "Mom, it's not bye, it's see ya later." My mother really saw at that time, as long as I've been telling her, I'm gonna do something about it, she saw that I meant it this time. But, you know, I had to quit on my own.

After 30 days in the detox center, she immediately went to New Horizons to receive long-term support to transition out of the lifestyle she had led for most of her life.

Roxanne's account draws attention to some of the hardships she experienced that colored her overall view of street-level sex work, including prolonged drug addiction. Similarly, most of the women espouse negative assessments of prostitution, often based on the many difficulties attached to it. This perception, in and of itself, does not generally pull them out of the trade. It many cases it is precisely these adverse circumstances and conditions, such as drug addition, that constrain their efforts to leave.

According to family studies scholar Rochelle Dalla, prostitutes leave the trade via three main avenues: jail, on their own without assistance, and via nonprofit organizations that serve this population.[1] In this chapter, I examine the process through which women initially exit prostitution as they enroll in a PSO. Prior studies explore various dimensions of this topic, including motives for leaving, a typology of exits, and different turning points that prompt this transition.[2] The analysis in this chapter extends this body of work as I highlight the relevant factors that shape initial exits—the first phase in the overall exiting process. I examine both the internal and external factors that bring about this break from the sex trade.[3]

Reasons and Motivations for Leaving

When asked, all the women in this study provided reasons for wanting to leave street prostitution. In fact, each individual provided at least two, with an average of 2.55 explanations per person. However, their accounts suggest that having motivations to exit is a necessary but not sufficient condition to this transition. There is limited social science research that analyzes reasons for leaving prostitution. Within this work, the following motivations emerge as salient: relational factors, restrictive factors (e.g., physical deterioration, sobriety), spirituality, cumulative burdens (e.g., hitting bottom), and being in a transitional context (e.g., jail).[4] These findings lay important theoretical groundwork for understanding the motivations for exiting, but tend to be insufficiently contextualized by the background and life experiences of the individual. Thus, in this chapter, I consider how unique individual characteristics, experiences, and biographical factors affect women's formulation of their reasons for leaving street-level sex work.

During the formal and conversational interviews with women, I asked a series of questions about how and why they left prostitution. One common motivation for exiting revolved around deeply held spiritual and religious beliefs, which was particularly prevalent among those who were raised in highly religious households. In short, they viewed exiting as a way to "get right with God." Marquietta, a 40-year-old who worked in prostitution for over 12 years, highlighted the important role her "higher power" played throughout her life, even while she continued to violate her religious tenets. She explained how religion was a prominent feature of her childhood and how her faith eventually served as a primary motivation to quit:

> My mom was a Jehovah's Witness and that's the religion I was raised in. I always had faith. When I was working on the streets I kept praying to God, "This is not me. Why do I keep doing this? Why can't I stop? God help me stop." He was always there knocking, I just had to open up the door to allow him to come in and help me stop.

Olivia, an African American who was raised Baptist, also viewed her faith as an ongoing process that ultimately became a central reason to exit. The following account sheds light on her thinking and her decision-making process:

> It's because I actually felt the hurt that I was putting up on the Heavenly Father and Christ. That was the ultimate straw that broke the camel's back. I promised myself I would never hurt them again and that gives me all the reasons more that I'm going to stop. The other reasons that made me want to quit—I don't like it no more, worry about going to prison, or for my kids—none of those worked though. It is God who gives me strength to make the choice to leave.

Women were also motivated to quit when they witnessed and encountered excessive violence during their time on the streets. Violence in impoverished urban contexts tends to be heightened, and research concludes that female street prostitutes experience particularly high rates of assault.[5] In a recent study on this topic, fellow sociologist Aaron Blasyak and I find women involved in street prostitution implement four types of protective strategies in their efforts to thwart violence and assault.[6] The effectiveness of using such tactics to reduce attacks, however, is still unknown. It is clear that these negative interactions escalated fears of future assault and death among women, and for certain individuals these concerns emerged as reasons to leave the lifestyle. Marquietta, in addition to having religious motivations, also pointed to the increased violence on the streets that became too much for her to bear:

> Really, I thought I was going to die in the life because I didn't see any way out no matter how much I wanted it to end. Things were getting worse on the streets day by day. I'd seen about five prostitutes I knew end up dead in garbage cans.

Stephanie concurred that the violence she experienced while in sex work was a major reason she wanted out. She explained:

> I was almost killed by my last john and I ran for my life. I knew I needed
> to get help but I couldn't stop. It was bad out there . . . I was raped many
> times and left for dead, having people cut my face up and damage my eye.

These traumatic experiences and fears were often exacerbated the longer one remained in the trade. And when experienced or witnessed firsthand, they frequently engendered feelings of exhaustion and perceptions of being too old to continue in this line of work. The prostitutes who referenced exhaustion and age as reasons for leaving typically worked in the trade for a large portion of their adult lives. Lily, in the sex trade for 15 years, claimed to feel the effects of the years on the streets, which for her served as a motivation to leave:

> I was tired of prostituting. Yeah, I wanted to try and change my life and I
> was having a hard time doing it [prostitution] anymore . . . So I came here
> to this program to try to get out of it and off of the streets, so I could do
> something else because I'm getting way too old for it.

Melissa felt that her 17 years as a sex worker had burdened her with many mental and emotional problems. She claimed to be exhausted from the work, and declared that most girls who leave prostitution are also motivated by this factor: "If they are really, really ready to change their lives [and leave], mostly it's because they are tired. That's the main reason you will hear the girls give. They are just burned out by the work."

Although uncommon, a few women stated that their sexual orientation served as an impetus to exit prostitution as it became increasingly difficult to have sex with men. For instance, Leslie had a disdain for intercourse with men because she was a lesbian. She said she first knew she was a lesbian at 14 and claimed that sleeping with men grew more despicable over time, and ultimately became a primary reason for her to quit:

> I just got tired of being with different men all the time. The smells, the
> touches, and all that stuff . . . I'm gay. To be with a man is really fucked

up to me. I'd always try to play my way out of the sex by either talking or
conning them. I did that very well.

All the women in this sample except one admitted they were addicted
to drugs while working in prostitution. As a result, money to sustain this
habit became a factor that kept them immersed in the trade. Once sober,
numerous women emphasized that the clarity and insight they gained in
turn produced a motivation to leave sex work. To that end, sobriety was
often a precursor that enabled women to identify their genuine feelings and
perceptions about working in prostitution. Rochelle, a routine user of PCP
and cocaine for 11 years, said her addiction kept her in prostitution and
after she was clean, she had no need to return to the streets. She recalled:

> My habit was basically what really kept me out there. So I think that when
> I really decided that I don't want drugs anymore that helped me with the
> prostitution thing. I don't need to go out there and sell my body because
> I didn't do drugs anymore and that is basically what I was doing it for. So
> now that I am sober I know that I can do without it. I got some insight.

Beverly attributed her mental breakdown to drugs, and claimed sobriety
was paramount for her to retain her sanity after a stint in a psychiatric ward.
She felt that working in prostitution was incompatible with a sober lifestyle:

> I never really thought about leaving before I came to the hospital, but I
> knew I couldn't get high no more because I would start hallucinating and
> all kinds of stuff. I was scared. I used the whole time I worked the streets.
> I think once I got sober, I got a moment of clarity and it dawned on me
> at that time that [prostitution and drug use] was not the way I wanted to
> die. Before being sober, I never had thoughts of leaving.

A desire to salvage damaged relationships with children or significant
others also served as a reason to exit. Approximately three-quarters of the
women had children, and for many, being able to raise their children, reclaim

custody, or simply reestablish a relationship with them was an utmost priority. Aretha had lost custody of her children years earlier and had little interaction with them, but she still wanted to protect them from potential negative encounters they could face due to her actions. She explained:

> I started thinking about my kids and that's why I first considered leaving. They are teenagers now and I would never hang around their neighborhood or hang around their friends because I was afraid that I was going to date one of them on accident. If that happened, I feared my kids' friends would tease them—"Hey man, isn't that your mom? Your momma sucked my dick." That would be horrible.

In addition to children, other interpersonal relationships with family members, partners, or close friends constituted reasons to exit. There were two main ways these relationships motivated women to leave the trade. First, when women considered their relationships with significant others too important to lose, their maintenance became a reason to quit. Hayley, a Hispanic 32-year-old, recalled her fiancée's disapproval of her lifestyle:

> When my fiancée found out I was prostituting he agreed with me that I needed to change my life. He didn't like the drugs, alcohol, or prostitution . . . basically the way I was living. So to be with him, I needed to change.

Hilda, an African American, also claimed she did not want to lose her boyfriend—also the father of her four children—as a result of prostitution and drugs because she considered him a "good man." In her case, he was unaware of her involvement in sex work, although he knew of her drug addiction. She felt compelled to stop both, since they were interrelated, before he found out and severed the relationship.

Interpersonal relationships, when they formed a mentor–mentee dynamic, also motivated women to leave sex work. In these instances women had relationships with former prostitutes who had successfully left sex work with the help of programs. Current prostitutes viewed ex-prostitutes as role models, as the latter extolled the virtues of their decision and served as living examples that such a transition was feasible. One 51-year-old client stated that she decided to quit after she witnessed two other women graduate from a PSO and thrive in their new lifestyles. She recounted this alteration:

> I saw the evidence through my sister and another lady in my neighbor-hood who were out on the streets [in prostitution] and doing really bad. I saw the changes in them after they went through the program and that's what helped motivate me to want to leave.

These accounts demonstrate that prostitutes often maintain multiple reasons to leave the trade, and they are rarely mutually exclusive. The above statements help contextualize individual motivations as they form from personal biographies and experiences. Understanding women's reasons for exiting sheds light on the internal forces that prompt this decision, but rarely do they result in an initial exit. Rather, it is a combination of personal motivations and turning points that occur within the individual that crystallizes her dedication to quit.

Turning Points of Change

While harboring motivations for quitting was a central factor that facilitated initial exits, women also emphasized a turning point event that elevated the salience of leaving. Indeed, turning points can cultivate a shift within a person that brings a new set of priorities and goals to the forefront.[7] Even as women cited multiple reasons for leaving, it was typically external events that produced a radical change in their thinking. Social workers Månsson and Hedin found three turning points connected to street prostitutes' exits from sex work: eye-opening events, traumatic events, and positive life events.[8] Similarly, for the prostitutes in this study, turning points consisted of being arrested, hospitalized, or getting pregnant, all of which can fit into one or more of the aforementioned categories. The effects of a turning point and the corresponding shift in thinking spurred women to gather information about ways to leave prostitution and consider available options for help in this endeavor.

The relevance of turning point events can be best understood by examining an individual's personal biography and life experiences. Criminologists Robert Sampson and John Laub argue that turning points are integral to role transitions out of crime.[9] In accordance, sociologist Peggy Giordano and colleagues stress that cognitive and motivational changes, such as turning points, are central to the desistance process for females.[10] My analysis concludes that turning points, coupled with motivations for leaving, indicate psychological and emotional readiness to embark on an alternative future life trajectory outside of prostitution.

Arrests and Jail

Given that street-level prostitutes are highly visible, it is not surprising that most of the women in this study had been arrested for prostitution at some point during their career. As a result, many served one or more jail or prison sentences. The prolific criminalization of street-level sex workers is well documented. Those who had a history of multiple arrests and extensive criminal records, in particular, spoke of their heightened fears of returning to jail and the prospect of serving long-term prison sentences. Faced with this reality, close to three-quarters of the women cited incarceration as a turning point event. Arrests and imprisonment subsequently removed women from street environments, instituted sobriety, and provided a space for personal reflection—conditions that cultivated turning points.

Recall Marquietta, who stated that her reasons for getting out of prostitution consisted of religious beliefs and intense fears of experiencing violence on the streets. However, these motivations alone did not compel her to exit, as it was not until she was rearrested and returned to jail for a period of time that exiting became her primary mission. She explained how her imprisonment was a turning point event in her life, one she attributed to God:

God finally rescued me the last time I went to jail, and it finally clicked after I was arrested that this was God's way of helping me out. I prayed for God to strengthen my faith in him and to put him in my life . . . To feel what I knew was right and what I was raised to believe in. I embraced that and ran with it because that was my lifeline and I knew with no doubt in my mind that if [I] would have kept going the way I was going, I would end up dead. After I was released, I went right into the program because I knew this was my one shot.

Desiree, a prostitute since she was 11 years old, had a substantial history of arrests and jail time and had recently violated her parole. Although she provided multiple reasons why she wanted to leave the streets, such as accomplishing personal goals, her rearrest and the prospect of long-term incarceration elicited a turning point change within her. She described the circumstances:

I was on parole and I got busted for prostitution again. I knew I was going back to prison for a long time, so I called my parole officer and asked her to recommend me for Phoenix instead. At that point, I knew something had to change. I got lucky. Instead of returning to prison, I got a chance to go there.

Rochelle, who claimed that maintaining sobriety was her primary reason to quit sex work, did not attempt to do so until she was arrested and faced a long stint in the penitentiary. She declared:

I had a rap sheet long—from here to El Paso probably. I was arrested for drugs and prostitution. And all my misdemeanors turned into felonies. I knew I was going to do some serious time in the penitentiary—at least three years. My public defender advocated I go to a PSO instead and I took it. At that moment, I knew it was time to make a change.

These cases emphasize the relevance of particular events—such as arrests and incarceration—as they serve to motivate individuals and also bring about a change in thinking (e.g., turning points). For those who had a history of involvement with the criminal justice system, including multiple arrests, imprisonment, and lengthy criminal records, it follows that the prospect of future arrests and long-term incarceration engendered a turning point in their lives, when the costs of remaining in prostitution became too high.

Hospitalization

Another event that cultivated a turning point for prostitutes was when they experienced intense psychological duress that resulted in hospitalization. In these situations the women attributed their change in thinking to their time spent in the hospital, where they were able to gain clarity, take stock of their situation, and formulate alternative lifestyle options. Approximately one-quarter of the women cited their hospitalization as responsible for producing a turning point moment.

Even though Beverly had a variety of reasons for wanting to leave prostitution, it was only after she entered a hospital due to a mental breakdown that she made the decision to exit. She felt that her mental instability was a result of her drug use, which she attributed to the difficulties of sex work. After this realization, she felt she could not return to the streets:

> I never really thought about stopping [prostitution] until the drug thing really took a toll on me mentally. I started hallucinating and began losing my mind and it wasn't fun. That's when I really wanted out. When I was in the hospital I recognized that this was it—now or never. Something clicked inside me.

Olivia also suffered from mental illness, which she blamed on her heavy drug addiction, and ultimately attempted to take her own life. Her motivations for quitting encompassed a spiritual awakening; however, it was not until her hospitalization that she gained insight into her lifestyle, which ultimately catalyzed a willingness to take the necessary steps to exit:

I tried to smoke myself to death, drink myself to death, and take pills and had to go to the psychiatric unit for six days. It was during this time that I had the clarity to know that I needed help. When I was released I came right to this program.

The prostitutes who experienced a psychological breakdown usually attributed it to their intensive and prolonged drug habits, which they claimed were necessary to cope with the difficulties of the work. After being hospitalized for treatment, they experienced a turning point where they believed their lives (and sanity) were at risk if they returned to street prostitution. Thus, they felt the only way to prevent further damage and/or death would be to radically alter their lifestyles.

Pregnancy and Childbirth

While uncommon, the final type of turning point was brought on by pregnancy and childbirth. Lily, who had six children, was one of the two women who claimed that pregnancy became a turning point in her life, causing her to reprioritize her behaviors. Shortly after giving birth, her main goal was to leave prostitution so she could be a mother to all her children and especially to her newborn son:

I want my kids back. So that's basically another reason why I got out of prostitution. I realized it was time to stop when I was pregnant with my son and I didn't want to be doing that anymore since he needed a mother. At that point, I started trying to figure out how I could leave and what else I could do instead.

Other women mentioned restoring their relationships with their children as a reason to quit, but only two women discussed childbirth as a turning point that elicited fundamental shifts in their thinking about their work.

A Change of Heart

Turning points were central to initial exits because in spite of harboring reasons to leave sex work, these prostitutes did not have a profound change in thinking before they experienced one of these events. It was arrests and jail time, hospitalization, or childbirth that altered their priorities and goals and subsequently produced a commitment to drastically change their lives. As Aretha declared, she would never have left prostitution if she had not experienced a change of heart while in jail. Beverly concurred: "No, I never previously thought of leaving prostitution, and if it had not been for my going to the hospital, my social worker and the program, I would still be out there today or probably dead." Even when women decided to quit, they usually did not know how they would achieve this outcome. After their turning point moment, and a change in thinking, women began to investigate resources to help them leave the trade or they were encouraged by an outsider to do so. PSOs served as avenues through which they could accomplish this goal. However, in order for a PSO to be perceived as a viable option to exit, prostitutes first had to learn about the program and what it offered.

Entering a PSO

In addition to internal factors, external conditions also help cultivate an initial exit from sex work. One such factor is based upon prostitutes learning of a PSO as an avenue through which to leave. Indeed, knowing about a program and the services it provides can increase the appeal of exiting and make it appear attainable, as one can expect certain provisions through this relationship. I find prostitutes either had short- or long-term knowledge of the existence of a local PSO. A majority of women had short-term awareness of a PSO (three months or less), which they acquired during the process of entering the program and typically through a bridge party. The remaining women retained long-term knowledge of a PSO (over three months) yet did not enroll until much later—an average of two years among this sample.

Individuals who carried long-term knowledge of a PSO but did not enroll for a lengthy period of time acquired this information through various methods: by using PSO programs and services, through staff of affiliated institutions, via family members or friends, or through media exposure. PSOs that offered particular services—drop-in crisis shelters, street outreach services, and jail outreach services—spread the word about their organizations through these channels. By providing an array of services, PSO staff members had numerous avenues through which to disseminate information about their programs to street prostitutes and cultivate interpersonal relationships with them.

For instance, Aretha first heard of New Horizons when she began using their temporary crisis shelter years before enrolling in the program. She explained:

> See, I was just a crisis client coming in and out, getting meals or sleeping. Because I knew that if I joined their residential program, then I'm gonna have to do the right thing. But at that time I wasn't ready to quit.

Other clients stated that they learned of the existence of a local PSO while working on the streets due to interactions with staff in a mobile outreach unit. Program street outreach typically focuses on distributing safety measures (e.g., providing condoms) for sex workers, establishing relationships with prostitutes, and providing information about how to attain other types of needed services. Beverly said she initially found out about New Horizons via staff members who worked in the street outreach program:

> I had always known about them as far as passing out condoms and stuff on the streets . . . I even knew them on a first-name basis. But did I go in for the help and all that? No, I did not. I even lived really close to the residential house, but I never once thought about going there because in my mind there was no help for me.

Another way women discovered a local PSO was through social work-ers affiliated with other institutions, such as jails or hospitals. Olivia stated that it was her hospital social worker who provided details about Safe Place, a PSO she had never heard of previously. She recalled how he presented it in a positive light:

> I was in the hospital for eight days and the social worker, Mr. Green, came and spoke about this program. He said it was peaceful and there were counselors there that could help me, and all that . . . that was about two and a half years ago, and that's how long it took me before I actually ended up here. But it was at that point that the seed was planted.

Other women found out about PSOs through their family members or friends. Derica attributed learning about the program through her sister and a fellow prostitute, both of whom had enrolled years before:

> I had seen the evidence of the program through my sister, who graduated from the program a few years back. And another lady in my neighborhood was also a prostitute and really bad off. She went to the program too and they both did well. They're now out of the life.

A friend in jail told Hilda about Phoenix for the first time. She clarified:

> I heard about it at least a year and a half ago from a friend while I was in jail. She went to the program before, but I guess she didn't do what she needed to stay out [of prostitution] because she was back on the streets and in jail once again.

Finally, women also acquired information about PSOs from advertise-ments or articles published in local newspapers. Around the same time she learned of the program from her friend, Hilda also saw an article in the newspaper about the program. The article included an interview with the program director, described the history of the program, listed the services they offered, and contained their contact information. She cut out the article and kept it for future use. Similarly, another client came across an advertisement in a local paper that she claimed "stuck in her mind" for years. During our discussion, which was years after she read the ad, she verbally recited the headline that resonated so strongly with her: "Do you want to get out of the life of prostitution?"

Although a minority of women possessed long-term awareness of PSOs, this knowledge alone did not engender a transition out of the trade. Instead, the information was mentally stored away until they were ready to act upon it at a later time. In contrast, the women with short-term knowledge of PSOs learned about them during their enrollment process. While women had a variety of motivations for leaving, experienced turning points that placed exiting as a top goal, and, in some cases, even knew of PSOs for substantial periods of time, most still did not exit the trade. All of these factors were important components leading up to enrollment in a PSO and at least a temporary break from prostitution. Yet in almost every case, a bridge person was crucial to make this transition a reality.

Third-Party Bridges

Third-party bridges are individuals who maintain detailed knowledge of a PSO, share that information with female sex workers, and facilitate their enrollment within these organizations. As bridges they not only inform the women about PSOs, but often use their social or professional positions to make the transition smoother. Research on social networks refers to this third-party bridge as a "broker," an actor that mediates exchanges between two other actors not directly linked. Based on sociologists Roberto Fernandez and Roger Gould's conceptualization, the two types of brokers are representatives and gatekeepers, where the first group's interests are aligned with the supplier (e.g., PSOs) and the latter group's interests are allied with the customer (e.g., the prostitutes).[11] These concepts help illustrate the different types of bridges that connect prostitutes to PSOs. I rename the bridges that have aligned interests with the PSOs "professional bridges," because they are largely motivated to connect the two parties based on their professional duties or obligations. Alternatively, I refer to the bridges whose primary interests lie with the prostitutes as "personal bridges." They perform an integral role in connecting prostitutes to PSOs and facilitating their enrollment within a short time frame. Past research on this topic pays little attention to these third parties or their relevance to this process.[12]

The most common professional bridge parties that linked women with PSOs were individuals associated with the criminal justice system, including public defense attorneys, parole officers, and police officers. These brokers informed prostitutes about the program, and, based upon their power, advocated for this sentence in lieu of imprisonment. Ultimately the judge decides the final sentences for female offenders; however, attorneys, parole officers, and even police officers can affect and shape these outcomes. Desiree was a client who first heard about Phoenix through a chaplain while in jail, and shortly thereafter asked her parole officer to plead with the judge for her placement there. As a bridge party who had substantial influence over her sentence, it was up to her parole officer's discretion whether she would be able to enter the PSO. Desiree recalled the sequence of events:

> I heard about the Phoenix the third time I went to jail through a chaplain who told me there are programs for prostitutes. I've never heard of one before that. At that point in time when she came to me I had no hope. Because I did a crime—prostitution—I was on parole. I was looking at 18 months at least in jail. I didn't know if I was going to get into the program, not because they wouldn't accept me but because my parole officer wouldn't recommend it. I had to go through her first. So I called my parole officer and I told her about the program, but I didn't know if she would recommend it for me or not. Finally, she did and I was able to enter.

Rochelle also stated she first learned of a local PSO when her defense lawyer suggested she try to get accepted. He set up a meeting between her and the program's director to see if she would qualify, and subsequently advocated for Rochelle's placement in this program in lieu of a lengthy prison term. She explained:

> When the public defender said, "I know a long-term program, I'm going to give the director a call, and she's going to come up here to interview you and see if you are eligible," I said okay. I was ready to quit, I was tired, and I was looking at three years in the penitentiary. Luckily, I got in and I am now a proud program graduate.

Aretha, who knew of the PSO for years, finally enrolled in it because her lawyer, upon her request, pleaded for her to be placed there rather than serve prison time. Like Desiree, Aretha also depended on a professional bridge party to recommend placement into a PSO. She was quick to emphasize that she wanted to go to the program because she knew it was a "life-threatening situation" for her, where she would likely die if she continued working on the streets.

In rare instances, the police served as the bridge between street prostitutes and PSOs. Even though the police had no authority to force a woman to enter a PSO, in circumstances where a woman was willing to accept their suggestion they became the effective bridge. Lily, whose last pregnancy and infant son became her turning point, needed a bridge party to tell her about the program and then help her enroll. When she was too exhausted to work and collapsed on the ground, the police officers who found her carried out this role: "The cops picked me up and they brought me here, and that was the first time I heard about this program. I thought the program wouldn't take me but they did because the cops knew the director. I've been here ever since."

Social workers also functioned as bridges, and were instrumental for prostitutes who experienced traumatic events, suffered psychologically, and landed in the hospital. For example, Beverly emphasized the important role her social worker played in getting her into New Horizons after she wound up in a psychiatric hospital:

It was a social worker from the hospital who got me to go to the program. She asked me, "Is this the way you really want to die?" I think in the midst of that encounter I got a moment of clarity, and it dawned on me it was not. So it was that little conversation with that social worker that finally got me here. She set it up so when I was released I came straight here.

Olivia shared a similar story, where she was in a psychiatric hospital after she attempted suicide, and a social worker recommended Safe Place, which she had heard of years earlier. After receiving the suggestion and experiencing a turning point, she finally felt ready to attempt a lifestyle change and allowed the social worker to orchestrate her placement into the program.

Lawyers, parole officers, police officers, and social workers all acted as professional bridges because they shared a mutual interest with the PSOs, which was to get women out of prostitution and cease their involvement with the criminal justice system. Moreover, acting as brokers between prostitutes and PSOs provided benefits for these workers professionally, as these placements could potentially fulfill occupational goals and demonstrate their job effectiveness. As one police captain declared:

We [the police] became an advocate for this program, not only by distributing information to the prostitutes who we were directly involved in the criminal justice system, but also to other agencies, such as courts. You know, if we could keep her from going on the street again by connecting her to this program, we've not only helped her, but we've accomplished our goal for the community as well. I think it works as a real good win/win situation for both of us.

All the professional bridges developed formal relationships with their clients, as their occupations focused on promoting citizens to adhere to laws, remain out of crime, and be self-supporting. Thus it was in their best interests to get women to leave the streets and quit sex work with the hope that many would permanently implement these changes.

Family and friends also were bridges between prostitutes and PSOs. These individuals served as personal bridges whose interests primarily aligned with the prostitutes due to their interpersonal relationships. Derica first learned of the PSO a few years back and only decided to actively pursue exiting after she experienced a turning point while in jail. Upon this realization, she turned to her sister, a PSO graduate, for help in her placement:

> I went to call my sister and asked her if they will help me. I asked her, "Will they have a spot for me?" She told me more about them, provided their number, and put in a word for me with the director. I called them and they said as soon as you get released you can come. I came right here from jail after my sentence was done because I knew I couldn't do it alone.

Shawnta admitted a friend became the crucial link between her and Phoenix when her friend provided informing about the program, including their contact information. She explained:

> The director of the program would go to the prison and give presentations about the program, what you had to do to qualify, and so on. So a friend I had in jail saw that, kept that information, and would pass it on to other women in jail who wanted another chance at life but only those who were serious about it. After we became friends, she told me about the program and gave me the phone number. I called them and told them I heard about it through a woman who met the director in jail, said I sincerely wanted to quit prostitution, and asked for an in-take interview. They granted it and admitted me. Once my sentence was up I came right in.

The personal bridges did not have professional incentives to facilitate prostitutes' enrollment in PSOs. Instead, it was their affective, close relationships and general desire to help these women that fueled their actions.

For only a few women, there was no bridge person who facilitated their entrance into a program. These women were extremely self-motivated to acquire help from a PSO, and after gaining awareness of their existence, they took the necessary steps to secure a spot in the program.

For instance, after learning about Phoenix, Hilda took the initiative to get enrolled by persistently calling and checking back with staff members until she was accepted. She described this process:

> And I called and they told me that they didn't have any beds available. And two months later, I called back and she was like we don't have any available now but call me back in a week. And I called her back again and I got one. At that time I had been out of jail since August of last year and I waited all that time, hoping to go there. Why? I was ready to change my life. It was worth the wait.

Regardless of the length of time they knew about a PSO, a large majority of prostitutes relied on professional or personal bridges to facilitate their entrance into a program. Despite a variety of motivations, bridge parties orchestrated the placement of prostitutes in PSOs as they felt these programs would help facilitate their exits from sex work.

Embarking on the Exiting Process

Rather than argue that there is one prominent explanation that accounts for a woman's initial exit from sex work, I conclude that it is the combination of internal and external factors that generates her placement in a PSO. Certain factors are internally based, such as personal motivations for leaving and experiencing a turning point event that altered her priorities and goals. Indeed, these accounts illustrate that motivations and turning points do not randomly materialize, but often emerge from one's personal biography and experiences. The remaining factors—learning of a PSO and bridge parties—were external to the individual, and therefore, largely depended on other social actors. However, when women acquired knowledge about programs from outside sources, they still had to perceive the PSO as a viable pathway out of sex work. Once they adopted this view, they usually relied on a third-party bridge to establish or condone this arrangement. For some women, this placement was entirely contingent upon the bridge's permission and advocacy. It was the intersection of internally based cognitive and emotional orientations *and* external actions committed by others that ultimately pulled women off the streets and into PSOs. A prostitute's entrance into a PSO indicates the first phase in the overall exiting process.

In chapter 2, the women discussed the difficulties of working in prostitution and stressed they had few resources or supportive networks to draw upon, grappled with addictions, and typically lacked direction about how to change their lives. Thus, many felt they would not be able to successfully transition out of prostitution without aid and guidance. For the women in this study, this help took the form of a PSO. Although people certainly leave prostitution without the support of programs, these sex workers believed PSOs were integral in facilitating their exits from prostitution and transitions into conventional lifestyles. The following account by Leslie illustrates this perception, and underscores her dependence on organizational direction and resources.

> Yes, I couldn't do it alone. I tried to quit before but it didn't work. I started to get back on drugs. Or I'd find myself in a predicament that I couldn't handle and I needed money. Or I would be staying someplace and they would tell me that I had to get out. Where was I going to go? The only thing I knew was to go and get money from men [through sex] and once I started doing that I started using drugs again, too. The program offered me a different way out. I knew they helped you get an education, a job, and maintain sobriety.

Rochelle also felt Phoenix could teach her how to live a life outside of prostitution, something she was unable to do on her own. She clarified:

> So I knew it was just time to stop and I didn't know how and I felt that this place was definitely going to show me how. They provided me with so many tools I didn't have or couldn't get on my own. They offered me an education so I could get a job and support myself.

Beverly stated when she was ready to leave she did not know how to accomplish that goal alone and turned to New Horizons for help:

> I didn't know what I wanted at the time, but I did know that I didn't want anymore of what I had been getting. I knew something about the program from the street outreach, and I knew they had a structured program set up that could really help me. The structure of the program was key to teaching me some sort of responsibility so I could take care of myself without relying on prostitution.

In a final illustration, Derica admitted that she was unsure how to exit prostitution because her life was so chaotic. She realized a PSO could facilitate this transition because she had seen its success by observing the radical changes in previous clients:

> I thought about leaving a million times. I just didn't know how. When my life was a total mess, I knew that for me to get some type of self-worth I had to come here. Because I saw what the program did for my sister and another lady I knew and the changes they went through, I felt it had to be doing something right. I decided to commit to this program.

In short, many women believed they could not exit prostitution on their own. They felt that utilizing the services and resources of a PSO would expedite their transition off the streets, provide them with structure and teach them skills, and ultimately improve their chances of success. Initially leaving the trade and entering a PSO is an important step toward accomplishing this goal; however, this act is only the beginning phase in the overall exiting process. Over the next few chapters I will explore the dynamics between the PSOs and the prostitutes immersed within them, as they influence whether women continue to progress toward leaving the trade or remain unchanged. I assess their headway by analyzing prostitutes' talk and behavior over time.

4

Getting On

Role Distancing

Beverly was a loquacious 35-year-old woman who had worked in prostitution for almost 19 years. During one of our many conversations she revealed the formidable circumstances she had experienced throughout her life, starting in her childhood. Her father was a drug dealer and pimp, and after her parents divorced when she was 10, her exposure to this deviant subculture was routine. After engaging in sex work at an early age, with her father's approval, she began a long period of criminality. When I first met her she had three years of sobriety under her belt and had not returned to sex work. Beverly discussed her past openly, in part to emphasize the changes she had implemented in her life. One illustration of this juxtaposition was when she quantified her 200 plus arrests during her tenure in the street life, which she referred to as her "rap sheet," and her desistance since that point. When I prompted her to elaborate on how her life was different now, she succinctly remarked, "I live a better life today because I don't live by the codes of the streets anymore. I now decline sexual propositions in exchange for money." This statement exemplified the phenomenon of women separating from prostitution and the culture that surrounds it, known as role distancing.

In the previous chapter, I explored the internal and external factors that resulted in female prostitutes' enrollment in a PSO. Yet the act of entering a program does not guarantee that a woman will quit sex work, because this initial exit is only the first phase of the overall process. This process is a temporal one and comprised of three phases of change. Once a woman is immersed within a PSO (phase one), I find that the organizational context and culture greatly influence the subsequent role exiting phases.

In this chapter I focus on the second phase of exiting prostitution, where women begin to display evidence of role distancing. Renowned sociologist Erving Goffman defined role distancing as "effectively expressed pointed separateness between the individual and his putative role."[1] I argue that PSO structures, attributes, and control mechanisms either facilitate or constrain role distancing among female prostitutes. Program clients indicate a separation from prostitution by displaying verbal and physical signals to those around them. Other studies demonstrate that role distancing is a strategy used by various groups of individuals—insane asylum inmates, the elderly, and the homeless—who want to deny their affiliation with that stigmatized or low-status role.[2] Prostitutes who engaged in role distancing were immersed within organizational settings that exerted pressure on them to do so through entrenched coercive and normative mechanisms.

While some clients enacted role distancing, others signaled very little separation from the role attached to prostitution and instead appeared to experience role conflict. Role conflict occurs for individuals when pressures and difficulties mount as they try to inhabit what they consider to be multiple incompatible roles.[3] This is apparent when clients' talk and behavior are contradictory, and they continue to exhibit traits or characteristics aligned with the subculture of street prostitution. Through interviews and field observations, I assess prostitutes' role distancing within four distinct PSOs, and shed light on the dynamics that unfold between the two.

Possessing a Stigmatized Role

Most individuals within society are eager to hold positively evaluated and high-status roles. By occupying these roles people receive external validation, praise, and a certain level of prestige—rewards that can engender high self-esteem and self-efficacy. Conversely, the opposite tends to occur for those who inhabit roles that society stigmatizes. Psychologists who study stigma claim that it can have profound and deleterious effects on the mental health of those who are stigmatized, often lowering their self-esteem and self-worth.[4] Street-level sex workers are a highly stigmatized population who tend to experience negative repercussions due to their affiliation with this social status. In chapter 2, I included accounts from street prostitutes that underscored their awareness of the low social position they inhabited. Moreover, their candid recollections provided insight into how this role produced internal conflict, negative emotions, estrangement from family and friends, heightened drug use, and deteriorated health for them.

In order to be stigmatized for occupying a deviant role, one must first be labeled and then treated as deficient by other nondeviant social actors.[5] This social categorization results in discriminatory practices enforced by the "normals" onto the "discredited" individuals, where the latter is mocked, ostracized, and often punished. Over time, the recipient internalizes the label and the associated negative connotations.[6] Street-level sex workers are visible to the public, which makes passing as a normal extremely challenging. Once labeled a prostitute, they effectively become what sociologist Howard Becker calls outsiders—individuals who are marginalized from conventional society and subsequently become more deeply entrenched within their deviant subculture.[7]

Of course, being a prostitute is not the only role that generates this type of undesirable social response. There are many deviant roles, and those who inhabit such roles typically experience negative outcomes as a result. Normative behaviors for women in our society continue to reflect pervasive essentialized notions surrounding gender, where women are largely expected to be virtuous, giving, nurturing, and sexually available but chaste. Although these norms are starting to slowly change—which makes new social positions and roles attainable to them—women in our culture are still measured by these gender expectations. Noncompliance opens up the possibility of repercussions, including stigma, denunciation, and labels. Despite some crumbling of the edifice of gender roles, women who work in the sex industry, and particularly in prostitution, arguably occupy one of the most highly stigmatized roles.

As a result of the damage inflicted by labels, stigma, and disenfranchisement, many street prostitutes are eager to express distance from the role.[8] This strategy is deliberate, since one is perceived to be a role incumbent unless he or she indicates otherwise.[9] In attempts to counter such assumptions, individuals must make concerted efforts to display distance from a deviant role to bystanders via their talk and behavior.

Role distancing is an active process, a strategy used by those immersed within undesirable roles to demonstrate a separation from them. Sociologists David Snow and Leon Anderson find that the homeless expend much energy on role distancing—from their roles, other homeless individuals, and the care-taking agencies that serve them.[10] Similarly, sociologist Marnie Sayles confirms the prevalence of role distancing among elderly nursing home patients, who attempt to reject that role by verbal disavowal, separating from other patients, and taking on alternative, high-status roles.[11] For both stigmatized populations, these techniques are only successful when outsiders validate their signals.

Even though there are many incentives prompting individuals to signal distance from a low-status role, only certain prostitutes across these programs performed it. Others were reluctant or refused to do so, and therefore, indicated role conflict. Role conflict occurs when pressures arise between the demands of several roles, and ultimately causes distress for the individual that affects how she acts.[12] When prostitutes displayed role conflict they exhibited inconsistency or contradictions in their verbal and behavioral cues, causing outsiders to question their intent to exit the trade and doubt their overall progress.

The phases of role exiting, however, do not unfold in a social vacuum but instead are influenced by PSOs. As I examine this second phase of role exiting, I pay particular attention to the attributes and mechanisms inherent in PSOs that either facilitate or constrain client role distancing.

The comparative nature of this study allows for such an analysis. I find that PSOs employ what organizational scholar John Van Maanen calls *tactics of organizational socialization*, which refers to the "ways in which the experiences of individuals in transition from one role to another are structured for them by others in the organization."[13] These tactics encompass coercive controls and normative mechanisms that emerge within organizational cultures. PSOs do not exhibit uniformity in this regard, but instead they vary considerably in terms of their implementation and enforcement of practices intended to elicit client changes.

Coercive Organizational Controls
Imposed Separation from Street Subculture

One organizational feature that cultivates role distancing among clients is a program's ability to physically isolate women from the subculture (and individuals) connected to sex work. Based on their structure and organizational policies, certain PSOs effectively implement this separation by offering prostitutes a residential setting where they can live for a set period of time. As their own entity, these settings have the ability to enforce lifestyle guidelines and daily routines for residents, which is often in marked contrast to their lives in prostitution. This practice is commonplace among organizations that aim to reform or "fix" people, as copious studies confirm they are designed to elicit client changes by instituting rigid rules and instructions.[14] New Horizons, Phoenix, and Safe Place were all residential programs that offered clients a place to live removed from drug use, prostitution, and crime. In contrast, the fourth site, Seeds, did not provide residential accommodations for women engaged in prostitution.

Street prostitutes work in an environment where their role is on public display; therefore, it is defined and labeled by outsiders, who in turn tend to ostracize them. Within this subculture, however, they interact with actors who occupy other deviant (and often criminal) roles, including pimps, other prostitutes, drug dealers, and the homeless. In order to leave the role of prostitute, one must cease interactions with her circle of supporting actors who help reify that social position and status. Sociologist Helen Rose Ebaugh refers to this as disengagement, which entails a person's social and psychological withdrawal from a particular group and the role that is enacted when interacting with that group.[15] Role distancing and overall exiting can be exceedingly difficult if the individual remains immersed within deviant subculture milieus.

Upon enrollment in a residential PSO, some women began to exhibit distance from that role, which was evident both verbally and behaviorally. The residential structures of New Horizons, Phoenix, and Safe Place enabled this role separation as they fostered client isolation from the outside world for a delineated period of time. These PSOs established daily routines for clients based upon scheduled activities and parameters for behavior. Across these PSOs, residents were unable to leave the premises without explicit permission from staff members or a chaperone until they had proved to staff they were trustworthy. As a result of this segregation from the outside world, bolstered by their restricted mobility, residential PSOs enacted coercive social control over their clients. If clients violated these restrictions, they were heavily sanctioned and frequently expelled from the program.

This was not only an organizationally condoned practice, as many clients also stated that the separation from their past associates and environment was a positive arrangement, one that helped them withstand the temptation to return to sex work.[16] Derica, a 49-year-old graduate of New Horizons, claimed the residential structure was integral for her to be able to leave the lifestyle of prostitution behind. While she admitted she missed certain individuals from her past, she believed they would impede her transition out of the trade:

> There are times now when I still miss those people [associated with prostitution] because some of them I was around for many years . . . but I know I cannot go around them no matter how much I miss them. It runs through my mind sometimes to try to reach out but then I always remember that ugly side and say, "Hell no, I can't go back."

True to her statement, Derica abided by these rules, avoided neighborhoods where she used to perform sex work, and relinquished contact with individuals connected to that role.

After enrolling in New Horizons, Felicia declared she could not return to the neighborhood where she worked because everyone there associated her with the trade and treated her accordingly. She confessed that reverting back to prostitution was a possibility and that it still held some attraction for her. Therefore, as a novice in the program, she felt it was in her best interests to cut these ties. Her account reflects her separation from that role, which she attributes to the insulation provided by New Horizons:

> I had no other associates or friends that were clean or out of the lifestyle during that time [shortly after entering the PSO]. So if I left New Horizons and went back to my old neighborhood, even to visit, I don't think I would have got out of prostitution because it was too tempting for me.

Ericka, a 40-year-old client, also appreciated the limitations on her physical movement. She stated that the residential facility was one of the best things about the program because it granted her a reflective space where she could focus. She characterized it as a peaceful setting that allowed her "to get herself together without being surrounded by all that outside pressure."

Many Phoenix clients felt similarly, and compared the residential setting to a safe place: a home. For example, Rochelle affirmed that the live-in facility was a major asset of the program: "The environment was great. We weren't institutionalized and although we were in a program, we were in a home." Hilda, who worked in prostitution for five years, stressed the importance of being in such a highly regulated environment. She clarified: "Because I need to be around this type of environment, that's gonna, you know, teach me things and help me . . . a better environment than I was in before. I could always get drugs and things right away where I was before. But that is all removed here and I'm removed from it."

As a residential program located in a remote rural area 30 miles from the city, Safe Place offered the greatest physical (and symbolic) separation for its clients. The distance and lack of easily accessible transportation not only deterred women from leaving the grounds, but also simultaneously encouraged their disassociation from street acquaintances. Many found the quiet, natural setting peaceful, and a welcome contrast from their chaotic urban lifestyles. Olivia, a client who was soon to graduate, explained how the location helped her attain a state of calm, which in turn gave her the insight she needed to experience personal growth: "The program has helped me because I feel the peace and serenity that I didn't feel in the city element. Here you have the basic needs in life and you are detached from things of your past, which allows you to grow and change as a person."

Another Safe Place client, Stephanie, who had worked as a prostitute since she was a teenager, also remarked on the benefits she derived from the rural residential facility: "I like that it is away from the city and the hustle and bustle. It's serene out here and that allows me to calm down and think clearly for once so I can put the past behind me." These accounts imply that for many it was easier to mentally, emotionally, and physically separate from prostitution and signal that to others after being immersed within a residential program.

Provision of Resources

Residential programs not only ensure women a physical separation from street subcultures, but they also encourage role distancing by alleviating clients' financial dependence on sex work through the provision of housing, food, and other amenities. According to some scholars, these services may ameliorate the structural conditions that often keep women immersed in the sex trade.[17] As reflected in the above statements, after entering a residential PSO many clients expressed great mental and emotional relief due to these provisions. They can also, however, function as coercive controls because in order to continue to receive them, women must abide by the organizational rules and expectations or run the risk of losing them.

Recall the excerpt from Beverly at the beginning of the chapter. She also praised the residential structure and amenities of New Horizons, because it granted her the space to be able to reflect on her life and gain some distance from prostitution. She mused:

> You know since being here I've learned a lot of things. I live a better life today because I don't live by the codes of the streets anymore. I now decline sexual propositions in exchange for money. When I first came in I didn't know what I wanted at the time, but I did know that I didn't want any more of what I had been getting. It was the structured program set up that really helped me to talk about some things that had happened to me and what life was like when I was on the streets. I was able to tear down some fences and build some new ones and I was able to begin to see myself in another life. A lot of that was because the structure the program gave me, and all the things they offered, such as housing, food, job training . . .

Similarly, Melissa, a Phoenix resident, directly linked the program's provisions with her ability to leave sex work behind: "Phoenix is an excellent opportunity for prostitutes who want to leave. You don't have to pay rent. They can go to school for free. Even all their books are paid for. So with these things available you can really focus on changing."

Evie, a 38-year-old, also stated she could direct her attention to leaving the street lifestyle because of the amenities Phoenix provided its clients. When she was asked whether the program structure and services made things easier for her during this transition, she unequivocally stated:

> Yes, especially the fact that they are paying for everything: housing, food, eventually school through donations and all that. And they supply a driver to take me wherever I want to go, like school or doctor's appointment. I don't need a car. So they are making things as easy as possible to get a different life. So I can actually concentrate on my studies when I go back to school and do something else.

In contrast to the three residential PSOs, Seeds, which was organized as a class and quasi-support group, did not grant these resources to clients.

When the women desired these amenities they were instructed by staff members to seek out state-sponsored sources of aid. The Seeds program lasted for a two-week period, which clients attended Monday through Friday from noon to 5:00 p.m., and contained one cohort of women per cycle. After the class ended each evening, most women returned to the crime-ridden neighborhoods where they worked as prostitutes. Many resided in transitory housing, stayed with family or friends, and some were homeless. In all these cases, Seeds clients continued to surround themselves with individuals who reinforced their role of sex worker via routine interactions, because the program did not provide a live-in facility that imposed a separation between the two worlds. And although staff members encouraged clients to cease contact with these individuals and eschew such neighborhoods, there was no practical way to enforce this and the women had few resources to relocate.

The juxtaposition between these two disparate worlds took a toll on most Seeds clients, and typically manifested itself as role conflict. Ongoing encounters with boyfriends, customers, other prostitutes, and drug dealers when outside of the PSO dampened their ability to carve out and sustain distance from that role. Gabriela, a 31-year-old African American, was struggling to separate from the role of prostitute as she navigated these contrasting environments. One day she arrived to class and admitted to the staff that she had spent the weekend with her boyfriend at his mother's house where everyone was using drugs. She candidly stated that she also used drugs and turned a trick that weekend to earn more money, a behavior she connected explicitly to her addiction. She stressed how difficult it was to be immersed within a setting where people were high and drugs were accessible when trying to remain sober. Melanie, a Seeds staff member, responded: "When you start using drugs you start doing other things you aren't supposed to, like prostitution. You can't keep associating with your boyfriend if he uses. You need to dump him and start taking care of yourself." Despite Melanie's admonishment, the reality of the situation was that Gabriela had no other immediate alternative housing options where she was shielded from these temptations. On a few occasions she tried to spend nights at the local homeless shelter, but found that drug use was just as rampant during the night hours.

Shortly thereafter, in another illustration of role conflict, Gabriela unabashedly regaled the group with the following encounter she had had the previous evening while shopping with her boyfriend: "I was with my boyfriend at the mall and I waiting outside his car in the parking lot for him to meet me back there. Three different tricks drove by and propositioned me. I didn't do it even though I really needed the money. I knew they were undercover cops." What is striking is that Gabriela's account did not imply role distance, but rather it implied that she did not engage in sex work because she was "smartly" performing her trade in order to avoid arrest.

Another Seeds client, Bella, shared Gabriela's concerns about her neighborhood that was rife with drug use and prostitution. She recounted the following story in which she was confronted by an old associate who was "high as a kite" as she was waiting for take-out food at a local restaurant. The friend offered her drugs but Bella refused and told her she was now sober. She quickly fled the area and the interaction. As a result of these encounters, she claimed it was exceptionally taxing to have any contact with her old friends and acquaintances now that she was in the program, attempting to maintain sobriety, and refrain from sex work, since they fortified that deviant role for her. But it was challenging for women to entirely avoid former associates, because they inhabited the same community.

Compared to the other three PSOs, Seeds' organizational structure offered clients limited physical, mental, and emotional separation from prostitution because it did not provide a residential shelter that sequestered them from the street subculture affiliated with sex work. Consequently, this organizational feature made it more difficult for clients to experience and express role distance from prostitution given that they were still immersed within a context where other social actors continually reified that role.

Rewards and Punishments

In the prior section, I discussed a common practice across the PSOs that offer housing for clients: The women are prohibited from leaving the premises without staff approval or a chaperone. The presence of this

policy reflects a similarity between residential PSOs and total institutions, which are notorious for being environments that impose strict
rules onto their inhabitants and regulate most aspects of their lives.[18]
Beyond physically removing prostitutes from environments that may
entice them, selective PSOs applied other methods of coercive control
to encourage role distancing among their clients. One took the form of
staff assessment of client talk and behavior that generated either rewards
or punishments for them. Staff members carried out the onus of the
enforcement of PSO guidelines and subsequently bestowed or revoked
benefits, depending on each woman's compliance. Their evaluations were
fairly straightforward because the organizations instituted clearly defined
behavioral parameters for clients. New Horizons and Phoenix fostered
organizational cultures where substantial coercive control, via both physical isolation and rewards and punishments, was endemic.

When clients (including Hilda, Stephanie, Beverly, and others) displayed talk and behavior that implied role distance from prostitution,
staff members perceived they were altering their lifestyles and growing as
individuals. Thomas, the chief program officer of New Horizons, defined
client progress in the following manner:

> You can see it in terms of them becoming more empowered to make the
> decisions, more accepting of the guidelines of the program, compliance with
> the criteria to transition to another phase. And you see it when they come in
> through orientation not wanting to adhere to a lot of the guidelines to get-
> ting to phase two and three . . . to hear them actually really having goals and
> seeking employment and taking the GED, discussing getting back with their
> children, proud of having six or seven months of clean time and talking about
> the things that are healthy for them. I think that's when you see progress.

Even though staff members did not conceive of these acts explicitly as
role distancing, the talk and behavior that Thomas described imply a
separation from prostitution and the subculture attached to it. Once a
client spent some in the PSO (minimally three months) and showed

compliance to its rules, New Horizons and Phoenix rewarded her adherence in the form of a day pass off the premises to visit approved family members or partake in chaperoned group social outings sponsored by the program (e.g., to movies or local fairs).

The case of Hilda, a mother of four, illustrates this quid pro quo. She had been at Phoenix approximately six months before she was given permission to visit her family outside the facility without supervision, and it was at her nine-month marker when she received her second pass. After a visit with her children for a few hours on one of these excursions, she returned to the residential house with a broad smile on her face and in an upbeat mood. When a few other clients expressed their envy of her day out, she reminded them she had worked hard to earn that perk.

Although clients are rewarded for condoned talk and behavior, they are also punished for their noncompliance to program expectations. I found that New Horizons and Phoenix used both the carrot and the stick as part of this coercive mechanism. Punishments consisted of staff denial of passes, additional chores, or rejection of one's promotion to the next program phase, which allots additional privileges to clients. Thomas elaborated on the discipline merited out for misbehavior at New Horizons: "We have consequences, level one through five consequences, and it varies. If it's something like using profanity it may be a day extra chore. If it's a level four they can possibly be discharged from the program. That can be from stealing to fighting or making threats, to drug use, or 'going out' . . . things of that nature."

Greta, the residential manager at New Horizons, also gave specific examples where a client would receive punishment:

> It depends on what the rule is and then that will decide what level of consequence they'll get. For instance, if they come in late to a meeting or group, or not completing a chore, or them being disrespectful to staff. They can get anywhere from extra days in kitchen duty, because they all hate that, or denial of a pass if they are at that point. We learn to take away what they love most because they don't want you to take it away and it helps them comply.

Janine, the case manager at Phoenix, described how staff reacted to clients who acted and talked in ways that violated program policies:

> We don't tolerate conflict, especially if it gets out of hand. Recently, we asked one resident to leave because she got into several extreme verbal altercations with another resident. During the last one, she threatened the other person, so that was too much. They also get passes revoked, too, for misbehavior or their allowance withheld.

Indeed, the staff members at New Horizons and Phoenix regularly corrected and punished untoward talk and behaviors, which they sometimes referred to as "street" manners. When asked to clarify this term, staff members listed disrespectful language (e.g., cussing), negative attitudes, aggressive interactions with others, violence, manipulation, lying, excessive flirtation with men, and dressing inappropriately.

In illustration of one such interaction, Ma S., the house manager of New Horizons, admonished a resident to modify her talk and actions:

> I keep telling one woman in particular that she shouldn't be walking like that and talking like that anymore, cussing and sashaying around the house. She is just using that street style talk and behavior, and she shouldn't be like that anymore, especially now that she's in the program. She's been behaving better since I came down on her.

Ma S. felt that it was her duty to facilitate these changes in women and enact discipline when she believed it necessary.[19]

I observed the following contentious interaction between a staff member and resident at Phoenix, where the former withheld allowance in an effort to affect change in her. Paula, the residential coordinator, was having an argument with Denise over hair gel, which she had purchased for multiple residents and distributed one bottle per woman. Denise was upset because she insisted both bottles were hers and accused the other client of stealing one from her. Denise's voice became louder, and she was soon yelling and condemning the other residents for being selfish and thieves. Paula attempted to correct her actions by stating: "This would be a good chance to extend an olive branch and peace offering to the other woman by sharing the gel with her. This would also give you a chance to learn a new way of doing things, instead of lying, cheating, and being deceitful to get what you want. You won't be getting your allowance next week." After allocating her punishment, Paula ended the debate by walking away.

Thomas of New Horizons underscored the importance of staff members' consistency and swiftness when they dispensed punishment for client misbehavior. He recounted the following example:

> Two women found a wallet in the house and one physically attacked the other over the money in it. We immediately discharged her from the program. We try to respond quickly and not let it linger . . . we have to adhere to the guidelines, hold them accountable for the consequence, and be consistent with it.

The dispersal of rewards and punishments was a common practice by staff members at New Horizons and Phoenix. The practice often resulted in client compliance with program sanctioned talk and behavior, which prompted the clients to signal to others their separation from sex work.

In contrast, Safe Place and Seeds did not have concrete policies or practices that resulted in rewards and punishments for clients. Rather, both programs offered few benefits for compliance, and staff members haphazardly and arbitrarily attempted to administer punishments in response to adverse client talk and behavior. Nebulous guidelines for clients and inconsistency in staff enforcement practices cultivated much less rigid organizational cultures, with little evidence of coercive social control mechanisms. Thus, these PSOs exerted much less pressure on clients to conform to their expectations, which were also amorphous, and resulted in few clients exhibiting distance from street prostitution.

Safe Place and Seeds offered very few client opportunities to achieve rewards due to their talk and behavior. For instance, Safe Place rarely allotted day passes to residents, where a client could leave the grounds unchaperoned, due to the short duration of the program. The three-month program did not typically allow enough time for women to demonstrate consistent satisfactory progress and elicit substantial trust among staff before they graduated. Safe Place hosted occasional group outings as a type of reward for select clients, but these were also exceedingly scarce events that were supervised by staff members. As a two-week program, Seeds did not offer either of these incentives for those who implied a separation from street subculture.

Beyond offering few, if any, rewards, Safe Place and Seeds also had unclear program rules and varying staff practices regarding discipline for miscreant clients. When asked about their program discipline, Kathy, the resident counselor and supervisor of Safe Place, admitted that the staff (and program) was lax on enforcing rules and discipline for clients. She described the typical program response when clients violated program rules:

> What we do is we will staff with that client. What that means is that a team of staff members will sit down with that client, and we would talk about her choices, what she learned from it, how she feels about it, what she would do differently. It's more of a working thing really . . . we're really not big on consequences here [she laughs]. We do have some consequences, but it's more about using them as a learning tool. For instance, we recently had one client who went to get her check cashed with a staff member and while she was in the bank she ran into an old dealer, made an exchange, and purchased, I think it was cocaine. The client then came back to the facility and used. Once staff found out, we talked with her about her choices, and strongly encouraged her to reflect on it in group sessions, what happened, why it happened, how easily it happened, what she could do in the same situation next time. Honestly, this client's been struggling to get engaged and involved in the program since that time and has really had a difficult time even completing those original directives. So another staffing was done with her to talk about that, and we said we noticed she is still struggling with these issues, and we want her to reflect more on the role of addiction in her life . . .

I asked Kathy if she thought this strategy was effective in eliciting changes in clients, to which she responded:

> No. Not as today, but I do think these talks are going to be extremely beneficial in the future for her after she's gone from here . . . at least I hope they will. The education that she's going to have to [use] at a later date when she may find herself in that same situation. You know, I'm all about education, and encourage them to ask and get as much information as possible so that whether they're willing to do it today or not, when the day comes, they're going to have information to [use] and make some better choices.

These undefined and extremely mild program consequences did not appear to facilitate client role distancing from prostitution. Indeed, many Safe Place clients violated program rules regularly by engaging in prohibited talk and behavior, faced few repercussions, and made little effort to signal distance from their street role. Nancy, a 33-year-old white woman enrolled at Safe Place, was extremely disruptive to the planned daily activities of the program, and created much chaos among the other members. Both her deteriorated physical appearance (an absence of most of her teeth) and volatile personality were attributed to her 10-year crystal meth addiction, which was financed through long-term prostitution. She showed up late to most mandatory classes, if she attended at all, and generally refused to partake in the discussions that centered on building a different life and leaving prostitution in the past. On multiple occasions, I was sent to look for her when she was absent from required activities and found her in her room or on the shared basement computer playing games. I reminded her that group classes were in session and she was expected to attend, and she replied that she did not feel like going. I left her and returned to the class.

Staff members did not punish her noncompliance beyond inquiring about her behavior during one-on-one sessions. A few weeks later, as she attended a group class, she raised her hand to speak. Nancy openly admitted she was having trouble changing and was not doing too well in the program. She claimed she did not want to die in the streets and needed to get her life straightened out so that she could take care of her three-year-old son. However, in spite of these proclamations, she continued to shun the other residents of the program and disregard most of the program activities and requirements. During a supervised group outing around this time—which in spite of her disregard for rules she was allowed to attend—she was caught attempting to buy and drink beer, a blatant violation of program policy. Again, she was not dismissed from the program but was asked to discuss her behavior with a staff member. Nancy's contradictory talk and behavior suggested very little role distance and instead indicated significant role conflict.

Seeds staff also admitted that the rules regarding discipline were not clearly outlined, and therefore could not be consistently enforced—with one exception. Because the clients who were enrolled in Seeds as part of their court-mandated sentence were required to take mandatory drug tests, failure of these tests violated their parole established by the judge. When this occurred they were asked to leave the program. This was not due to strict PSO policies, but rather attributed to those established by the state and broader criminal justice system. Besides this one strict policy, Seeds staff members did not have parameters concerning verbal and behavioral conduct for clients or disciplinary procedures that could encourage their separation from street prostitution. In fact, I found that staff members generally overlooked client street talk and behavior, as well as their blatant violations of most program policies.

Judy, Seeds' developmental director, stated that their program rules and disciplinary policies were still being ironed out, and typically it was up to staff facilitators' discretion to decide what client talk and behaviors were unacceptable. I asked her what happens when a client is unruly and disruptive to the class, and her response illustrates the subjectivity of the program rules and its lack of disciplinary measures:

> Like respect could be a rule, and so if that rule is broken then the facilita-
> tor needs to stop the group and address those rules and the need to keep
> those rules. And reiterate why those rules are in place. You know so there
> are some rules that have gray areas and there are some that are black and

white, like the drug testing. If they use, they are out of the group, and what happens depends on the structure of the court program.

Melanie, the lead educator and facilitator of the Seeds two-week program, provided a specific example of how she reacted to a client who challenged her authority, showed aggression, and refused to participate in the class discussions:

> Sure, there are times when women go off on me in class. One in particular was holding the group hostage with her attitude. And her attitude got nasty, and she didn't have her meds, and she was detoxing from drugs still. And by this time, she was completely unruly. One of the things I told her was first of all you are disrespecting the group and the women here, and secondly, I'm not going to put up with that behavior and if you want I can have you talk to the judge. But those threats didn't change anything because she still had the attitude for the whole two weeks, which affected everyone else there.

At Seeds, it was common for clients to indicate role conflict through their talk and behavior, a phenomenon fueled by their continued immersion within street contexts. A sign of this was a flat-out refusal to participate in the class activities. Maricela, a middle-aged Hispanic woman, was one of the individuals who showed little desire to leave prostitution or partake in the mandatory program exercises. On a few separate occasions, she interrupted the class by announcing that she was tired and was going to take a nap in the corner of the room. She got up, grabbed a blanket, and curled up in a chair in the corner during the middle of class. All the other clients observed Melanie, the staff in charge, to see her reaction. However, Melanie invoked no rules or reprimands but simply ignored Maricela and continued on with the class.

A few days later, Melanie asked the clients to set their future goals and Maricela remarked that God put her here for a purpose and it was not just to get high, prostitute, or sleep with just any guy. Yet later that afternoon during break, she told us she had sex over the weekend with a man she just met. The following is an excerpt from my field notes:

Maricela announced to the class that she got some action with Bones, a man she met at a local bar. She said she was having a few drinks when the cops entered the bar and because she didn't want to get accused of prostitution, she quickly left with Bones to return to her house where "one thing led to another." They had sex and she said it was great. Melanie asked if they planned on seeing one another again and Maricela smiled, winked at Gabriela, and replied that it was a "no strings attached" encounter.

The two present staff members immediately exchanged glances but did not respond aloud. After the class ended for the day and the clients all left, staff member Melanie told me she thought that Maricela was still working as a prostitute and that Bones was a client. The other staff member shook her head in agreement. In spite of their assessment, they made no effort to address this issue with Maricela directly or reprimand her for those behaviors. Altogether, Maricela made very minimal effort to display talk or behavior that implied a separation from prostitution; instead her actions suggest she struggled to remove herself from it.

Another Seeds client, Jessica, who is white, also indicated role conflict by her contradictory talk and behavior. During one class she espoused a desire to leave prostitution: "I want to change my life, do something else. I need to be a mother to my kid, and get my degree so I can be a nurse." A few days later another program member observed her in a car with a well-known customer, fooling around in the parking lot outside the building. The woman reported her to the staff, who then confronted her about the encounter. In spite of the eyewitness, Jessica defensively exclaimed that "nothing happened." The staff members allowed her to remain in the program and did not allude to the incident again.

New Horizons and Phoenix had clear, established rules regarding appropriate client talk and behavior, which enabled staff to implement a system of rewards and punishments. By enacting these measures, staff members were able to exert higher levels of coercive control over residents, which facilitated role distancing among them. Alternatively, Safe Place and Seeds had very few guidelines to regulate client conduct, and staff members did not uniformly or routinely allocate rewards and punishments. Even though staff made some attempts to encourage and reprimand clients, they were not codified into program policies, which in turn could have constituted an environment of continuity and structure. Instead, clients experienced less organizational pressure to exhibit role distance from sex work within loosely regulated settings.

Besides coercive control mechanisms, there are normative controls that affect role distancing from prostitution, including socialization between clients, socialization between clients and staff members, and time spent in the program. Although the organizational attributes and coercive controls help encourage client separation from prostitution, informal normative mechanisms also influence this practice.

Normative Controls
Fictive Families

In contrast to coercive forces of control, which are implemented formally at the organizational level, normative social control mechanisms are sustained through intensive informal socialization and interactions among program members. Programs that offer long-term residential services, such as New Horizons and Phoenix, maintain organizational cultures entrenched with multiple normative practices that encourage clients to leave the role of prostitute. Residential staff members are integral to the reproduction of these types of environments as their affection for clients produces a fictive family model for interaction, which in turn typically reproduces itself via client interactions.

Criminologists and sociologists who study women in institutional settings identify the importance of fictive families, as they organize and guide much of the social life within these confines.[20] This phenomenon has also been referred to as a quasi-fictive family, where counselors or staff members perform the role of mother (parent) while the members figuratively become the children (and siblings to one another). The cultures at New Horizons and Phoenix cultivated this type of familial atmosphere and corresponding socialization, as certain staff adopted the role of mother when interacting with clients.

In illustration of this familial milieu, the clients of New Horizons endearingly referred to the residential director as "Ma S."—a mother figure—instead of Mary. Derica did not perceive the intensive socialization and constant staff presence as oppressive; rather, she felt that their emotional and physical availability provided integral support that enabled her to cultivate distance from prostitution:

> One of the best things about the program is the staff being there, and knowing that someone was there 24 hours a day. It was the warmth, the understanding, the compassion of the staff that helped me change. In fact, when I was getting ready to leave the program I got really scared because I didn't have that secure blanket of people. I was terrified and Ma S. put me in her arms and rocked me and sang to me until I felt better. To basically tell me that it will be okay and I would be okay on my own.

Marquietta, five months at New Horizons, also expressed similar sentiments and claimed that the affection from staff members helped her leave prostitution:

> I love the staff. I can confide in staff very easily because I feel the love they have on a personal level. It's not just a job for them. I feel that it's way beyond just a job. They are doing it from the love of their hearts and not out of obligation, and it makes me want to reach out. When someone reaches out to you like that and you aren't used to having someone care for you from their heart it makes so much difference when you know it. You know when someone is really being straight with you or when they are doing it because they have to. And that's what makes me feel so close to the staff here because I know they are doing it because they want to do it, not because they have to do it. I like the time they will take out of

whatever they are doing to stop and talk to you when something isn't right or to encourage you when you are down. And they make it comfortable enough for you to talk. The different programs they have set up for you for going out into the world to prepare yourself to be something else . . . it's preparing you to make the next step into society. To be a different person.

Ma S. confirmed that these acts of affection were genuine, but she was also aware they helped engender changes in the clients as well:

> I give them a lot of TLC. That helps them and strengthens them. A hug here and there. I always call them on weekends and off shift if a girl is having a problem to see how she is. I tell her that she is special and I tell her, "I love you the best." I tell them all that. I really love them, I love them so much. I see them as my children. I just cherish the moments because you never know when one will walk out. When I leave and go home that's my greatest fear of coming back and one of my girls are gone. I cry all day long. I take it with me. With that attitude towards them it makes them strong too. They can feel that.

Similar to New Horizon residents, many Phoenix clients also emphasized that the care they received from staff members helped them disassociate from prostitution, which they attributed to the family-style program model. They especially felt the program director, Sally, was crucial to their transition out of prostitution, and like Ma S. at New Horizons, she served as a mother figure for residents. Melissa expressed her view: "Sally is like my guardian angel. So I guess there is a guardian angel over all women in prostitution. I feel like I could tell her anything and that support is so important to my recovery." Rochelle held a similar perception of the staff members at Phoenix:

> The staff was always there. You were never totally alone. If you had to talk you had someone there. My mom and I never got along before the program. I blamed her but it was basically me. But I felt that staff was the mother figure I never had. The things that we could talk about that I

couldn't talk to my mother about or wouldn't talk to my mother about I was able to talk to them about. Staff being there was a great help and still a great help to the women because a lot of them don't have mothers. A lot of them have been mistreated by mothers, and then they have this positive figure in front of them in Sally, that is like, "Oh wow." It's mind-blowing.

Sally, the residential director, verified the familial dynamics that existed between staff and residents were central to their organizational culture. She described it in the following manner:

> Yes, it's kind of an interdependence thing, where we are here when they need us. Kind of like our parents are there when we need them. I'm assuming that your parents are there when you need them as are mine. But I've learned that you can't always assume that. We kind of fulfill that role for these women.

Both New Horizons and Phoenix sustained program cultures suffused with this fictive family model—staff was routinely available to clients and lavished them with affection, support, and encouragement. Together, the staff investment in and client endorsement of this model facilitated the latter's exhibition of role distancing.

Neither Safe Place nor Seeds replicated fictive families within their organizational cultures, which was likely due to their short duration (three months and two weeks, respectively) and the staff members' unwillingness to take on such roles. While the staff members at these PSOs did offer clients encouragement and praise at times, none served as mother figures or nurtured them to the extent of staff at New Horizons or Phoenix. Safe Place and Seeds clients did not draw analogies between staff members and family, nor did they conceptualize their relationships with staff as familial or emotionally supportive. In short, these programs and their members developed different organizational cultures that felt transient and inchoate, resulting in much less intensive socialization experiences for clients vis-à-vis New Horizons and Phoenix.

Peer Socialization and Role Models

Peer-based socialization also occurred between PSO clients, and prompted women to engage in talk and behavior that demonstrated a separation from prostitution. Similar to the other mechanisms of control, the prevalence of peer socialization was heightened at the long-term residential programs due to their intensive and insulated program cultures in which residents were immersed for long durations of time. Moreover, the shared space, routines, and daily activities likewise encouraged strong affective bonds to form between clients because these programs offered a collective socialization experience.[21] This socialization was evident in the outward expressions of encouragement and praise between clients, when clients imitated the talk of role models, and in the disapproval clients expressed when others were recalcitrant.

Peer encouragement of one another was a common feature at both New Horizons and Phoenix, where residents vocalized their support of any changes that implied disengagement from prostitution and street life generally. Ericka, a New Horizons client, was in the program for five months when she stressed how the guidance and socialization with other program members enabled her to gain mental and emotional distance from the role of sex worker:

> Being around the other women in this program and getting guidance from them and staff helped me realize I can be different and am able to deal with the issues and behaviors I had when I was working on the streets. Before coming here I used to think of myself as an old crackhead whore and played the part. I don't think that way anymore.

In another example derived from my field notes, I observed an interaction between a few residents where two women supported another client and motivated her to accomplish her goal and strive for success. In this case, Marquietta and Patricia attempted to instill confidence in Roxanne about her ability to pass her upcoming driving test, a necessary achievement for her to apply for future jobs as a commercial driver. The following exchange transpired on one afternoon after a group session finished and residents were allotted a few minutes of free time:

> Roxanne was in deep discussion with Marquietta about how she feared failing her driving test, which she needed to apply for jobs. Marquietta reminded her she had plenty of driving experience so she was prepared. She patted her back and told her, "Don't worry, you'll be fine. You can do it. You'll pass." Patricia, another client, instructed her to "Take God with you tomorrow, he'll take care of it for you."

During another visit at New Horizons, a few residents sat in the living room on a brief break between lunch and a Prostitutes Anonymous (PA) meeting and chatted with one another. It was during this time that I observed Marquietta ask an advanced resident, who was known for being smart, to tutor her. Marquietta explained that she needed to brush up on her English skills and asked the other resident if she could help her study for her GED examination, to which she agreed. There was a lot of emphasis on educational attainment at this PSO by both staff members and clients. And indeed, educational attainment was an integral component to upward mobility for this population, as it elevated their chances of obtaining employment outside of prostitution. Perhaps more crucial, education also enabled them to divest from prostitution.

The comments from Shawnta, a six-month resident at Phoenix, also underscored the ways clients supported and encouraged one another to disconnect from prostitution. She identified one particular resident, Hilda, as someone she could trust, and therefore felt comfortable confiding in her about traumatic events that transpired while on the streets. When asked about the individuals who helped sustain her during this transition, she gave the following reply:

> My associates, my peers are really helpful as a source of support. Hilda especially. We have girl talks. Sometimes, there are things I don't feel I can

talk to staff members about because they haven't been a real-life prostitute. They don't always understand what it's like. So for those issues, I talk to Hilda and she will tell me how she truly feels about it. And it gives me a chance to weigh the options: Do I like hearing what she has to say? Does it have any truth to it? Can I use the information that she shares with me? And nine times out of ten something I can get from her advice is positive to help me move forward in my recovery.

Similarly Evie, a two-month resident of Phoenix, confirmed: "The best source of support are the other women here. Everyone that lives here has been really friendly and supportive. I haven't had any fights. I haven't had any arguments with people. That helps make this easier."

Although the clients at Safe Place and Seeds also occasionally engaged in peer socialization that prompted their withdrawal from the role associated with sex work, these types of interactions were uncommon. The following observation of two Safe Place residents constituted one of these sparse interactions. Stephanie, a Safe Place resident, was about to receive her first pass that allowed her to leave the property without a chaperone for a few hours one Saturday afternoon. I asked her if she planned on seeing any old friends during her pass, and she responded by describing a letter she recently received from a former friend: "One of my old friends wrote me a letter recently and asked if I was going to 'work' [prostitute] when I got out on my pass. I told her no! That really hurt me. Her assumption was so disrespectful that I cut her off and I won't talk to her anymore or see her again." Another nearby resident nodded her head in approval upon hearing Stephanie's story and commented, "Good for you, you don't need that bad influence near you. Focus on your future!" Her statement affirmed Stephanie's effort to disengage from prostitution. Generally, however, this type of socialization at either of these PSOs was rare.

Peer socialization was also evident when advanced residents or program graduates served as mentors for rookie residents. I noted the prevalence of these types of relationships at New Horizons and Phoenix, which transpired when role models and clients interacted with one another during scheduled group and class sessions, lunches and dinners, or down time. At both PSOs, the role models regularly visited the sites in order to teach classes, help out, give advice, or just socialize. Many clients relished these encounters, and because they perceived these women as successful, they began to emulate their talk and behaviors.

One African American New Horizons graduate, Sherita, led a class on how to boost self-esteem. In a verbal display of role distancing, she instructed the residents to change their perception of themselves: "I know now that my body is a temple and I don't give it to others especially for money because I respect myself. You shouldn't do that either." A few days later, I overheard a current client espousing the same phrase and sentiments to signal role distancing to those around her. Like Sherita, an informal mentor to the residents, she equated selling her body for money with disrespect: "I don't have a lot of great days going on yet, but I still feel good because I didn't go sell no pussy, I didn't go suck no dick, and I didn't go and get high. I can respect myself now by respecting my body."

Rochelle, a Phoenix graduate, also made it a point to spend time interacting with the current residents of the program. She was currently employed at a law firm, was living in her own apartment, had been sober for a few years, and had reunited with her family. She claimed that she wanted to give back to Phoenix and offer encouragement to the clients. When I asked how she did that, she replied:

> I make myself known. I make a presence. I appear. I try to be there when they are doing things, meetings or groups . . . when it's mandatory for them, if I'm there I do it too. It's the little things to show them that it's okay. I don't have to do this. I'm doing this because I like to show others that you can do this too. You can accomplish what I have. It's not hard if you put your mind to it. Humble yourself and accept that this [program] will not last forever. Accept you are doing this to change your life. Accept that you are doing this to better yourself to learn how to maintain a good life.

Throughout my fieldwork, Rochelle, African American, showed up once a week to spend a few hours with the residents and participate in on-site activities. Certain residents believed that routine interactions with role models were integral to their ability to leave prostitution. Melissa, a white resident 18 months into the program, felt that the one-on-one time spent with Rochelle was extremely helpful for her to transition off the streets. She recalled her conviction:

> Rochelle was here when I first came and then graduated. She now has her own apartment and is doing great. She has been my main support base besides staff. She gave me the inspiration to want to do certain things for myself, other than prostitution. When I first came here she was where I am at today. And I knew it could be done [leaving prostitution] by seeing women like her do it and following their footsteps. Basically, I am hoping that I can provide the same thing for the new residents that we have here.

Through their talk and actions, PSO graduates who served as mentors exemplified success and continued to display signs of distance from the role of sex worker. Organizational theorist John Van Maanen asserts that this relationship constitutes a serial socialization process, where experienced organizational members groom newcomers and serve as role models.[22] These routine interpersonal interactions prompted many current clients to imitate role models, enactments that indicated their own separation from prostitution. The organizational cultures at the other two PSOs, Safe Place and Seeds, did not engender the mentor-mentee relationships that helped spur role distance among clients. Moreover, peer-to-peer encouragement of disengagement was exceedingly rare at these sites.

Peer Disapproval and Shunning Techniques

A final type of peer socialization took the form of overt disapproval and ostracism of intractable women who did not verbally or behaviorally indicate disengagement from sex work, with the hopes of eliciting change in them. This method of control is not unique to female prostitutes who are immersed within PSOs. In fact, in a study on adolescent girls and violence, criminologists Meda Chesney-Lind and Katherine Irwin find ostracism and shunning commonplace, implemented to control and punish those who do not conform to prevalent social and cultural norms.[23] As it applies to female street prostitutes within programs, clients who enforce these practices are those who disassociate from sex work, while the recipients are primarily those who disregard these standards—namely those who exhibit role conflict. Alongside many of the other control mechanisms, this phenomenon was also most apparent at the two long-term residential PSOs.

Consider Aretha, a 42-year-old resident at New Horizons, who had been in the program for less than two months when she summarized her goals to me:

> To learn to be responsible, to be respectable, a respectable woman. I want to learn how to read and write and use proper language. I want to learn how to respect me before I can respect you and how to go to school before I can go to work. I need to learn how to stop being afraid of sober life and how to keep God first in my life. Most of all I need to learn how to stop thinking like a bitch and start living like a woman. Because I still be lusting over men, thinking "man I could do something with that" but it is just in my mind. I don't want to do nothing with them, I don't want no money for it, I'm just lusting.

Despite this stated desire for change, her daily talk and actions undermined its plausibility. Besides the above admission, she provided very few signs that suggested distance from prostitution and instead exhibited copious indicators of role conflict, where she still embodied the role of prostitute. I overheard her remark to another client: "I want to do well and get clean . . . to start over. But, then I'm scared because I just want to be out there with . . . that is all I know. I want to go back there [on the streets] and back to my life." Moreover, her routine isolation from the other clients and persistent refusal to participate in required group classes confirmed her reluctance to disengage from that role. In response, most of the other residents avoided her as much as possible because they felt she threatened to disrupt their own progress.

I asked Maria, a long-term resident, what she thought about Aretha's behavior, and she responded: "I don't like that some of the other residents don't seem like they get it. You know how serious this is, this is our lives and I need to stay focused when they are horsing around. I stay away from her 'cause I need to focus on myself and my recovery."

Aretha's actions underscored her hesitation—and even reluctance—to leave prostitution and that lifestyle. As a result, staff and other clients seriously doubted her commitment to exit. A month or so later she left the program after a prolonged heated argument with another client and staff member over her disruptive and antagonistic behavior. Her talk and behavior throughout her time in the program was a poignant example of role conflict, corroborated after she left the program when she was subsequently arrested a few weeks later on prostitution charges.

Phoenix resident Shawnta provided the following account of how she and the other residents shunned Denise, who was verbally and physically hostile to them and created much discord within the house. She described a recent argument over items at a yard sale that culminated in Denise's expulsion from the program. Shawnta summed up the sequence of events:

> It all started when we were having a yard sale at the house over the weekend. I asked Denise not to bring too many clothes to the yard sale because we had limited space. She didn't answer so I told her again, and then she started screaming at me to "shut the fuck up" and not treat her like a kid. But I was just relaying the message from staff. I walked away from her and stayed away from her all day. The next night during group, Denise brought up the incident and she started yelling at me, cursing me out, and finally threatened me: "I'm going to kick your ass!" She kept going on and on about it, in spite of the fact that staff were telling her to calm down and reminding her we don't talk like that here. The other residents felt sorry for me, and

we all decided afterwards to ignore her, and let her do her thing. I can't be around her. Now we all keep our distance from her to work on ourselves.

The impact of this type of informal social control at long-term residential PSOs was significant because the women were largely isolated from outsiders and were required to be around the other residents and staff members on a daily basis. Thus, they were subjected to considerable social pressure to comply with the cultural norms established within these settings. When I asked Denise about her feelings toward the other residents, she stated:

I don't trust them because they play kid games. He said, she said. They a clique. It's a little group. You know, junior high school shit. And I'm not into that. I don't need anybody to validate who I am. Because people have never done nothing for me. I've always done it myself. So I don't need any of these people to do anything for me, or tell me anything to make me feel good or fit up to their standards. I am who I am. I know what I'm capable of having. I know how to get it, like I've done all this time.

After a moment of reflection, she reluctantly admitted: "Well, I've lashed out since I've been here. To defend myself cuz I've felt threatened. I've learned that lashing out and cussing and getting ready to fight, physically violent is not the answer . . . that communication goes a long way." But in fact, her behavior was not in accordance with her talk, as she was asked to leave the program when she brandished a knife to threaten Shawnta days after their argument. With very few indicators of disengagement from the role she occupied on the streets, Denise continually demonstrated role conflict and appeared unable to leave that role behind.

Disciplinary socialization between clients was omnipresent and deeply ingrained within the cultures of New Horizons and Phoenix, and although I observed occasional glimpses of it among residents at Safe Place, it was atypical behavior. The few instances I observed at Safe Place included the following. Two residents at Safe Place, Annie and Nancy, often refused to attend required daily group classes. Instead, Annie hid out in her room and slept and Nancy was often in the basement playing computer games. Upon noticing their absence at group classes, staff members inquired about their whereabouts and instructed other clients and staff to locate them and command them to participate (which I described earlier). The goading—and at times, thinly veiled threats of punishment—had little effect on their behavior. I had an opportunity during one dinner to ask Annie, a white resident of Safe Place for less than one month, about her reluctance to participate. Her response highlighted her internal turmoil about leaving sex work and the associated culture:

> I don't know how I feel. Sometimes I want to be here and feel like I am at the point where I can do something different. Other times, I just want to get back to the streets where I came from and what I know, where I can get fast money and drugs. I'm just being honest because it's hard to go back and forth like that.

A few other residents were convinced they were "playing the system" and had no intention to change their lifestyle. Sandra complained that she was sick of the women who did not come to class when everyone else was required to attend. She elaborated, "It's not fair they don't come when we all do. But, I guess I'm just going to do what's best for me because I know this is helping me and by not coming they are just hurting themselves. They just aren't getting it. They probably never will." Later, I discussed the incident with another resident, Olivia, who also condemned their actions:

> Some of the ladies forget this is a treatment facility and not just a place to hide away. Because I see some women have a tendency to get too relaxed, and when I hear statements like "I don't have to go to class today," it irritates me to some degree because this is what we are here for. And I see they're going to feel the same bad way because they aren't growing and aren't doing the inner work needed to leave that old lifestyle behind. I do my own thing and ignore them.

Yet these Safe Place client reactions were sparse and had little impact on defiant program members. Finally, Seeds clients did not display any efforts to discipline or punish others who refused to express a separation from sex work. This is likely due to the extremely short duration of the program and is reflective of the norms within this particular organizational culture.

Formal and Informal Controls Impact Role Disengagement

Formal controls within PSOs intend to generate changes among their clients by the use of coercion, including restrictions on physical movement outside of the facility, the provision of resources and aid, and the institutionalized rewards and punishments. New Horizons and Phoenix implemented all of these forces of control routinely, which became embedded within their program cultures. Alternatively, Safe Place enacted some of these mechanisms, yet they were rendered ineffective due to inconsistent enforcement by staff and unclear consensus regarding the basic program policies for clients. The remaining program, Seeds, had only one formal control mechanism for clients—sobriety—for the duration of their time in the program. However, this rule was not generated or upheld by the program itself but by the external criminal justice system that subjected clients to daily drug tests as part of their criminal sentence.

On top of formal controls, certain PSOs sustained organizational cultures where various informal control mechanisms also shaped member talk and behavior. When present, these informal control mechanisms—fictive families and affective bonds, client encouragement and praise of one another, and peer punishments—pressured clients to conform to normative expectations. New Horizons and Phoenix were sites where these informal controls were omnipresent among residents. Safe Place, the other residential program, offered a much more lenient, relaxed culture for its clients where few forces of informal control constrained them. In comparison to the other three PSOs, the culture at Seeds was barren of virtually all control mechanisms, in part due to its extremely short duration, a feature that hinders the establishment of verbal and behavioral norms.

When implemented and practiced regularly, formal and informal social control mechanisms worked to urge clients to begin to separate from the role attached to prostitution. They exhibited this disengagement to those around them through their talk and behavior. This analysis stresses the importance of organizational contexts, as some PSOs possess particular cultures rife with control mechanisms while others do not. Program cultures include an array of organizational attributes, structures, rules, and policies, as well as socialization practices that encompass fictive families, role models, and peer disapproval. The cultures are generated and sustained through the organizational members, who often act as socialization agents. And although socialization occurs throughout one's duration in the program, and even beyond, its influence is most pronounced upon entry into a residential PSO due to this radical shift in environment.[24] Most clients begin to signal detachment from prostitution (and its subculture) within a short period when they experience enormous pressure to do so. Women are not only socialized within PSOs, but they often eagerly participate in it by holding others accountable for their talk and behavior. In doing so, this practice helped buttress their own efforts to disengage from sex work.

Women immersed within PSO cultures that did not have prominent social control mechanisms—Safe Place and Seeds—showed minimal or no display of role distance. They had little impetus to do so. Rather, there was ample indication of widespread role conflict among clients, where they struggled to disengage from prostitution and regularly acted and talked in accordance with that role.

As outlined in chapter 3, prostitutes may also have compelling personal incentives to desist, which can make them more amenable to coercive and normative forces of control. Pervasive control mechanisms can increase the salience of individual motivations to quit and thereby make women more likely to express disassociation from sex work. This analysis underscores the power of these forces within PSOs, as they can engender member changes.

Recalcitrant clients, or those who indicate role conflict, share some similarities that likely contribute to their stagnation: client modes of entrée (involuntary versus voluntary) and time spent in the program. These women were all court-mandated to attend the PSO *and* had been in the program for only a short duration of time, which limited their exposure to forces of control. In other words, their role conflict likely resulted from some combination of the following factors: a low prioritization of personal incentives to leave, involuntary enrollments in PSOs, and a brief time span in the program.

Involuntary modes of entrée may explain the reluctance of fairly new PSO members, yet this factor becomes less relevant to the exiting process over time because those who continuously engage in role conflict tend to fall out of the program. Similar to voluntary clients, the court-mandated women who do remain in a PSO for at least a few months tend to succumb to social control mechanisms and begin to signal a separation from sex work. This pattern raises the importance of temporality. Temporality can work to amplify the organizational and social forces that compel client role distancing. The longer one is immersed within an organizational setting where control mechanisms are widespread, the more challenging it is for her to resist them. Program duration is integral as it allows for ongoing and consistent socialization to occur—which not only puts pressure on clients to conform, but also fuels their internalization of ideal codes of conduct. Organizational and labor scholar Gideon Kunda argues that when normative control is effective within organizations, the members will be self-motivated to internalize and reproduce expected talk and behaviors.[25]

There is not a specific point in time when social control mechanisms take effect and engender client disengagement from prostitution. However, I find that women who consistently exhibit role distance have been in a PSO for at least two to three months. Those who regularly express role conflict are typically neophytes in the program (within the first month or two). The organizational structure and policies dictate the longevity of client immersion within the program. Recall that New Horizons and Phoenix were two-year programs, Safe Place a three-month program, and Seeds a two-week program. These program guidelines influenced client disassociation because they dictated the length of time one was immersed within a particular organizational culture. However, I find that formal and informal forces of control take precedence the longer one remains in the program, and eventually even alter the trajectories of those who involuntarily enroll in a PSO.[26]

5

Still Getting On

Embracing a New Role and Identity

In a conversation I had with Hayley, a Hispanic New Horizons graduate, issues of her changed identity and role emerged as fundamental to her transition out of sex work. She had completed the program four years prior and was busy keeping up with the responsibilities of her new lifestyle. According to staff accounts and her own admission, Hayley put in considerable work to overcome the many disadvantages life bestowed upon her: Her father abandoned the family when she was only three years old, her mother was an alcoholic, and as the oldest of four siblings, Hayley was forced to grow up fast. Her family was very poor and she often worried that they would be evicted from the cramped apartment that was the only home she knew. She recalled, "We were pretty poor but we never went hungry. My mom always fed us. As far as clothes, we got hand-me-downs from people that knew us."

As an adult, she struggled with alcohol and drug addiction, and after a drug dealer raped her when she was trying to purchase from him, she stated that something inside her shifted—she thought that if a man could take advantage of her then she would do the same by charging him for sex. Hayley began to regularly turn tricks to earn cash, which exacerbated her addiction to alcohol and cocaine, and soon she inhabited a lifestyle where sex work and drug use went hand in hand. She explained,

> I had to do it under the influence, I couldn't do it sober. So when I would drink [or use] that's when I would go out and prostitute. I did it every day.

But I never tried to stop . . . the cops would pick me up and take me to jail overnight and then I'd be back out there the next day.

During our interview at her apartment, I asked how she was doing and what her life was like after being out of the program for a few years. She admitted that the transition had been difficult at first, but she was now doing well. Her life now revolved around her fiancée, managing three part-time jobs, keeping sober, and being an active participant in her church. She expressed how she felt and in doing so alluded to the transformation of her role and identity: "Right now I respect myself and love myself. I love working and like what I'm doing. I'm ashamed for what I've done in the past but I can't change it. I can only look at the future. All I can say is that I don't ever want to go back—to the person I used to be." This excerpt from Hayley underscores the importance of this final phase of exiting, where the construction and embracement of a new social position (role) and sense of self (identity) indicate a radical lifestyle alteration for prostitutes. Altogether, these social-psychological changes serve as the bedrock for successful desistance and reintegration into mainstream society.

In this chapter, I examine how PSOs influence their clients' adoption of a new role and identity, and how clients' commitment levels facilitate this transformation. Renowned symbolic interactionist Erving Goffman defines role embracement as an "act where participants publicly embrace the ideologically defined member role as an authentic expression of their experience."[1] I find that anticipatory socialization is particularly relevant for clients as they move into this phase, meaning they must first distance from their previous role of prostitute as they prepare to embrace a new one.[2] This separation from prostitution also carves out the emotional and psychological space for women to formulate a new sense of self.[3] Two types of identity emerge as salient in this phase: One encompasses how individuals view themselves and the other is derived from outsiders' perceptions. These constitute personal and social identities, respectively. The former is imputed to oneself in terms of personal attributes, or the meanings an actor assigns to his or her self.[4] The latter is based upon our positions within structured social arrangements and identifications with socially constructed groups or categories.[5] Put simply, individuals tend to construct their own personal identity while external actors impart social identities to individuals, often based on the role he or she occupies.

Existing research concludes that role and identity changes are observable through one's talk and behavior.[6] Due to high visibility and the deeply entrenched moral assumptions about their work, street prostitutes' personal and social identities are often deleteriously affected by their role.[7] Social psychologist Jenna Howard claims that those who occupy dominant roles within society more easily sustain positive social and personal identities vis-à-vis individuals who are in stigmatized or low-valued roles.[8] This stems from the close connection between roles and identities, as role status is tied to social identity and therefore often informs one's personal identity.

When it comes to crime and deviance, sociologist Howard Becker posits that labels—ascribed social definitions that impute a certain social identity—have the power to negatively affect an individual's sense of self.[9] It follows then that the embracement of a new, prosocial role and identity may be especially challenging for those exiting lifestyles of deviance and crime given the high levels of societal stigma and marginalization they have likely experienced. Criminologist Shadd Maruna found that English offenders who desisted constructed a prosocial identity where they participated in conventional activities, contributed to their community, and subsequently received validation for doing so. However, this theory points out that they were able to maintain this identity, compared to persistence criminals, because they engaged in willful, cognitive distortion—essentially, they adopted an exaggerated sense of purpose and an unrealistically high perception of control over their lives that did not align with their reality as ex-offenders.[10]

Work by sociologists Giordano and colleagues also highlights the salience of cognitions as they cultivate identity changes among criminal offenders during the desistance process.[11] Their study illuminates various cognitive transformations that generate this shift, including envisioning a new self and the decreased relevance of the deviant lifestyle.[12] During desistance, they assert that offenders cognitively "begin to fashion an appealing and conventional 'replacement self.'"[13]

These studies help us gain a clearer understanding of desistance by linking cognitive changes to identity transformations, which help sustain this transition. Building off this work, my analysis suggests that the roles individuals inhabit cannot be divorced from their identity formation. In other words, in order to exit sex work prostitutes must experience cognitive changes that engender a new identity *and* also engage in behaviors that uphold an alternative self and role. I previously explored this interdependent relationship in an article on female prostitutes in the process of leaving the trade.[14]

The Impact of Prostitution on One's Identity

Almost all of the women affiliated with these PSOs claimed a personal and social identity of prostitute based upon their role, which usually became their master status. A few noted the positive benefits derived from this recognition, typically experienced early on in their careers. Derica was one of these women. She admitted that tangible markers of financial success colored her feelings about her identity: "Sometimes I felt really good when I made enough money. It made me feel great. When I didn't make enough money, I felt really bad and sometimes I made enough money and I still felt empty. I just felt icky on the inside doing what I did. Mostly, I didn't feel good about me." Over time, however, her earnings were unable to assuage the flood of negative feelings about her sense of self.

In general, by the time women enrolled in a PSO this identification overwhelmingly produced negative emotions and disparaging self-perceptions infused with shame, failure, and worthlessness. One woman summarized this view: "Yeah, prostitution had a big impact on me because I couldn't look at myself in the mirror. I was disgusted by what I was doing and who I had become." Lindsay from Seeds agreed: "It [prostitution] had a big impact on me. I was a doormat. I was used up."

Similarly, it was common for community members and the public to assign deviant, low-status social identities unto them for their participation in sex work. This label was especially difficult for clients to bear when family members and close friends conferred it. Being the recipients of a deleterious social identity often reinforced negative self-perceptions that infiltrated their personal identity. Hayley, a New Horizons graduate, recalled the shame she felt when her family observed her at work on the streets: "Yeah, my brother saw me one day when I was on the street. He told my family and my mom and they all disowned me because of that. I was too ashamed of what I did so I didn't try to talk with them about it or anything but just stayed away for a long time." A Phoenix client also described how her personal and social identities were acutely affected by prostitution:

> You turn off all your emotions, but then in reality all your emotions aren't turned off because you still have to deal with who you are and what you've done and how you were raised. There is so much embarrassment and degradation and after you have been out there for a while you start hearing things and people walk by you and talk about you. Even little kids teased me and called me names.

Marquietta, who had been out of the lifestyle for five months, succinctly described her social identity based upon her experiences with outsiders: "From society's way of looking at it you were nothing." When probed whether this influenced her personal identity, she confirmed: "Yes . . . I would look at myself in the mirror and become disgusted with what I saw—I was a dressed-up garbage can." Bella, a Seeds client, was extremely upset by how people treated her based upon her social identity. It was clear this assignment shaped her personal identity:

> It lowered my self-esteem. I felt no good, I felt worthless. I felt this was never going to end. I also felt unworthy of having the blessings that God has given me—that was to live, to have a family, to have two little girls of my own. And every time I looked in the mirror my self-esteem came down more and more even though I had a lot of guards up. I was always

angry, furious. It mattered because people would look at me differently, especially a lot of people who knew me. They were like, "You bitch, you ho, come suck my . . . " It hurt.

Ericka, who worked in prostitution for 10 years, shared the following perceptions and feelings about her identification with sex work:

My family and everybody knew. It hurt them tremendously, but, you know, I was sick and that's the way I thought at the time. I felt bad though. Especially when my father knew. Yeah, cuz he put me on a pedestal, you know, and it broke his heart. I know it did. And that affected me bad.

Marleen, a white Safe Place resident, also internalized the stigmatized, devalued social identity people attributed to her while she was in the trade: "I called myself an outlaw because that's what I was during all that time."

In response to the unfavorable identities generated from sex work, many women cope by relying on drugs to assuage their feelings of shame and despair. Past social science research has shown that prostitutes often turn to drugs as coping mechanisms to offset negative self-perceptions.[15] Amanda, a New Horizons graduate, provided insight into how drugs altered her emotional state in order to offset how she felt about herself: "When you are out there in your addiction, you don't feel anything. You feel like you are on top of the world and you are in control but when you come down you feel nasty and disgusting." Ruthie, a Safe Place client, explained that her drug use escalated drastically once she began working as a prostitute. Her statement implies that substance abuse was a way she attempted to mitigate the damaging impact of an adverse sense of self: "I think it was the shame and guilt I felt . . . I felt so bad about myself. The drugs helped me to escape from reality even if it was a brief, fleeting moment, and I enjoyed that." Jacqueline, a prostitute for 25 years, vehemently proclaimed: "Prostitution degrades women and takes your self-esteem. You feel disgusting if you are sober and you do it. So then you just numb yourself with drugs so you don't have to think about it or feel it." Finally, Beverly, African American, was introduced to the lifestyle by her father, who operated as a pimp. She explained how this role shaped her identity:

> You know, it really, really started to weigh on me especially in the end. It really impacted and affected me really bad in the end toward the last five years because then I really felt the dirty feeling you know. And I felt worthless as a person . . . the price kept changing and going down. By the end, I was down to 10 bucks and that was something that I never would have taken early on. In the last five years, it really started to bother my self-esteem, how I felt about myself, what I thought about myself.

For those who initially entered prostitution to support their drug habits, their addiction often intensified as a result. I discussed the prevalence of drug addiction among prostitutes in chapters 2 and 3, but above I establish the relationship between their deviant identity and drug use. These accounts suggest that engaging in prostitution significantly shaped clients' social and personal identities. Their ascribed social identities, based upon this role, were laden with stigma, derogatory characteristics, and low-status. Eventually this identity became internalized and influenced their sense of self (personal identity). Both types of identity ultimately elicited feelings of shame, degradation, low self-esteem, despair, and disgust within these women.

Embracing a New Role and Identity

Certain studies conclude that individuals who transition from a deviant to nondeviant role and identity are able to capitalize on this former affiliation in order to qualify for a conventional social position. An example is found in the research conducted by sociologist J. David Brown, which emphasizes that the experiences of former addicts made them especially qualified and well suited to become professional drug counselors.[16] This opportunity is unlikely available for most individuals who occupy deviant, criminal roles because we know that labels, stigma, and a history of crime usually place them at a disadvantage in mainstream society. In regards to prostitutes, there are very few opportunities for them to use their work history and experience as credentials for professional, legal employment. Given the extremely high taboo regarding street prostitution, sociologist Teela Sanders describes how former prostitutes tend to hide their history of sex work from others after they leave the trade.[17]

During the process of exiting, many women displayed talk and behaviors that indicated their embracement of a new, prosocial role and identity. The following excerpt from my field notes illustrates this phenomenon. After one afternoon class ended at New Horizons, Roxanne and I were the only two who remained in the living room. We began talking, and Roxanne, the oldest program resident, asked if I wanted to see pictures of her family. I agreed and she took me to her room where she pulled out a shoebox stuffed with snapshots from under her bed. As she thumbed through them and recited each person's name and relation to her, she confided in me about the embarrassment and shame that still weighed on her due to her involvement in prostitution for over 38 years. After a moment of silence, during which she stared intently at a picture of her youngest grandchild, she disclosed that without the help of New Horizons she would probably be dead on the streets. In the following excerpt taken from my field notes, she draws a clear distinction between her identity as a prostitute and her current identity:

> This program is so important to me because they brought me from being a little girl—I was a baby when I was on the streets—to being a grown woman now. I don't have to crawl around on my hands and knees or be on my back for nothing no more, like I did when I was a prostitute.

Not only do her words demonstrate her identity shift, but her behavior also provided further evidence of this alteration. She completed her chores on time, routinely attended off-site GED classes, mentored new residents, faithfully attended all group sessions, and had plans to attend a culinary program after she graduated the program. Roxanne remained sober throughout this time and was diligently moving through the program phases toward graduation.

The Impact of Control Mechanisms

While Roxanne's lifestyle changes are impressive, PSO clients did not experience identity and role transformations in a social vacuum. In chapter 4, I examined how specific control mechanisms facilitated clients' symbolic, physical, and cognitive distance from the role (and identity) of prostitute. I similarly find that forces of control impact their adoption of a conventional role and identity. At the same time, individuals immersed within organizational settings do not simplistically acquire new identities and roles, but instead tend to negotiate them.[18]

Previous sociological and criminological research examines social controls within institutional contexts, particularly as they prompt personal transformation or rehabilitation within members. These studies vary in their conclusions.[19] Some argue that rigidly structured settings fundamentally mold residents' identities while others highlight the ways in which individuals resist institutionally sponsored identities.

One illustrative study conducted by sociologist Ruth Horowitz finds that both outcomes can occur.[20] She analyzes a program designed to help teen mothers gain educational attainment and acquire jobs so that they are able to transition into adult roles. While she brings to light program control mechanisms that often produce subservient and subordinate statuses and identities among the young women, she does admit they are not always successful, as some girls repudiate such prescriptions. Her study underscores how organizational pressures can generate a myriad of client responses—often complex and contradictory—regarding their role and identity transformations.

The analyses in this book chapter extend this area of research as I identify particular coercive and normative control mechanisms present within PSOs that encourage such alterations, and explore the variety of responses clients have to these pressures. I also emphasize the agency of the women by considering individualistic factors, such as temporality and commitment levels, which also impact their willingness to move into this final role-exiting phase.

Coercive Control Mechanisms

Many of the coercive control mechanisms outlined in chapter 4 not only promote role distancing among clients, but also cultivate their embracement of a new role and identity. These include the organizational practices of removing prostitutes from street environments and the establishment of rules governing client talk and behavior, which are enforced through staff implementation of rewards and punishments. Organizational researchers John Van Maanen and Edgar Schein refer to this as the divestiture socialization process, an organizational strategy that disconfirms the entering identity of the recruit by isolating him from those who uphold that identity.[21] This type of organizational socialization seeks to deny and strip away certain personal characteristics of a member in order to rebuild a self-image based upon new assumptions. I argue that divestiture socialization, an organizational practice, was deeply entrenched within New Horizons and Phoenix.

The highly structured environments, as well as abundant and consistently applied rules and regulations at New Horizons and Phoenix, fostered settings where role embracement and identity change were expected for clients. This atmosphere and the watchful eyes of staff members exerted considerable pressure on residents to comply. Interestingly, many clients lauded these very controls for eliciting their transformations. Felicia, an African American New Horizons graduate, claimed that the program structure and regulation were crucial to her adoption of a new role and identity. She summarized:

> I was able to tear down some fences and build some new ones while I was there. I was able to see myself in another life. And I think it was just the way that the program was set up, you know, everything is structured, which gave me some sense of responsibility. For instance, if I left and said I was going somewhere, then I needed to be where I said I was going and I needed to be back on time or there were consequences, whereas before I never lived by no rules. That has really helped me to be a different person.

And, indeed, Felicia's prosocial role and identity revolved around her behavior: a conventional occupation as an administrative assistant in an architecture firm, her sobriety and participation in a 12-step program, and interactions with a newfound supportive network of friends. She classified herself as "extremely happy" in her life post sex work, and attributed much of her success to the program.

Beverly also credited her transformation of self to the program structure at New Horizons. The program emphasized responsibility and accountability to others, how to live according to rules, and basic skills that would help maintain structure in her life (e.g., cooking, routine bathing, conducting an interview, writing a resume, showing up for appointments). At the time of the interview, she had spent close to 22 months in the program and was in the process of transitioning out of the residential home. The following statement suggests that she not only embraced a conventional role, but also believed she was a different person:

> I am a diva now [she laughs]. You know what I just love me today and I just try to treat myself as such. I've learned a lot of things from this program and I live a more precedented life today. I don't live by the codes of the streets anymore and my life has changed tremendously. I'm fully self-supported now, and declining outside contributions [she laughs]. I just take care of me today. But I try not to ever forget where I came from and who I was because I'm not going back . . . I do that one day at a time. So much is new to me now, being a single mother and raising my son, having my own apartment. I got a whole lot of appreciation for my life today. I think the program made a pretty nice woman out of me.

Rochelle, a Phoenix graduate, found work as a legal assistant. Although she no longer lived at the facility, she was a regular visitor at the premises. The staff and other residents spoke of her with great affection and anticipated her frequent visits. She felt she was doing service by mentoring current residents, and claimed she wanted to be a living example of what could be accomplished with the help of the program. Rochelle emphasized that the structure of the program was important to the formation of her current role and identity associated with this altered lifestyle:

> Yes, without the structure and doing something constantly you have no motivation. You are just like a lump on a log. So I think the structure they gave is crucial—the motivation to get you up to go to school, the motivation to do chores, and it also teaches you that you have to earn money not go out there and sell yourself. You can do this. You can live off of $10. You don't have to have $1,000 a night. You can maintain: you can live. I'm proof that it works. Today, I work full-time as a legal assistant at a law firm. Everything is going well. There are no complaints. I feel like a different person. I'm sober and clean, and I am responsible now. The bad days I have now I wouldn't trade them for the bad days I had on the streets. Trust me. These are nothing compared to what I've been through. It's like a slap on the back. That's it. It's a trip I used to get high for any reason. But now, you know, the sun came out. But it took prayer, determination, and motivation, and Phoenix helped me in so many ways to become who I am today.

Pamela, the executive director of New Horizons, also underscored the importance of such changes in her remarks: "The change in clients is kind of like a metamorphosis. When they first come in they are this diamond in the rough, and then by the end, they are completely different people."

Phoenix staff members present similar organizational goals for clients that encompass shifts in their identity and role. Janine, the case manager, explained that a transformation within a client occurs when they "recognize they don't need to do this [prostitution] because they are worth more and are better than this." She continued, "We try to teach them to be functional in the world, where they can get a job, get up each day, and go to it . . . basically to be spiritually and emotionally happy and productive women." Felicia, Rochelle, and Beverly all noted that the highly regulated structures at New Horizons and Phoenix helped them implement lifestyle changes that ultimately led to their embrace of a conventional role and identity. Although clients may not interpret these organizational practices as control mechanisms, they operated as such.

In comparison, there was no such emphasis for clients at Safe Place and Seeds. As noted in the preceding chapter, neither were highly structured programs, leading to a lack of organizational clarity in terms of the expectations for clients. The rules for the women were not typically codified, and therefore arbitrarily enforced by staff members. These practices spawned organizational cultures that did not place a premium on client adoption of an alternative role and identity, which is reflected in the absence of divestiture socialization at both sites. Lacking this organizational impetus, few women at Seeds and Safe Place actually talked or behaved in ways that implied identity or role shifts.

Olivia, African American, was one of these rare individuals. When asked if she thought she had changed while in the program, she affirmed: "I would see myself now as coming complete, you know, my life coming out of the holes. I'm not the same person I used to be, no one close, no one close." However, in her discussion of identity transformation, she attributed her changes to self-will and determination rather than to the program. Indeed, she lambasted Safe Place for its lack of rules, structure, and inability to enforce and regulate resident behavior overall. Olivia vented that the staff could be firmer with clients in order to "let the ladies know this is a treatment facility and not just a place to hide away."

Kathy, Safe Place counselor and supervisor, confirmed that the staff had minimal expectations for clients, and exerted little pressure on them to demonstrate role and identity change. Her comments in the following excerpt encapsulate this organizational approach:

> You know, success for some women, that's going to mean they've increased their self-confidence, it's going to mean that they feel very motivated and excited to go out and maybe get a job or attend a meeting. Whereas for another client it may mean that they now have a better understanding of what addiction is, it may mean that they got their Social Security number, and they're going to have a safe environment to live in and not have to be

on the street. It may be that during their time here they simply start to participate more in groups or if they start giving feedback or even presenting something to the other client. So we view it on a very individualized basis here based on where they are when they come in, and who they are, and what direction they need to be going in.

With an even shorter program length, Seeds staff admitted that they hoped to just "plant a seed of change" within the women over the two-week program, but had no specific goals for them. As Judy, the research and development director, stated: "The major changes are up to the women to make by themselves after the program." Cynthia, a white Seeds graduate, described how most participants perceived the program: "I don't think most women took it seriously. And that's how they ended up back in prison. Most women looked at it as taking the easy way out rather than do the work [to change]."

Staff at all four PSOs admitted that the extent of client identity and role changes varied considerable. However, New Horizons and Phoenix were the only programs where divestiture socialization was a key feature, and a priority among staff members. They expected their clients to become different people while immersed within the program, and strongly encouraged them to do so. It was perhaps easier for these two programs to develop such a goal, and a culture that reflected it, given that they bore a close resemblance to total institutions with long-term treatment for clients. Seeds and Safe Place, on the other hand, were much shorter programs, and therefore unable to exert as much organizational influence over the women who utilized their services.

Normative Control Mechanisms

Normative control mechanisms also facilitated client embracement of a new role and identity. These informal practices consisted of mutual monitoring, role modeling, and affective bonds among clients. They were typically instigated and upheld via more advanced program residents. Normative controls were deep rooted within the long-term, residential PSOs, such as New Horizons and Phoenix.

Hilda, a nine-month resident at New Horizons, made it clear she no longer identified as a prostitute, in part because she no longer occupied that role. While she usually greeted me with a bright smile, one Thursday our paths crossed and she looked agitated and upset. When I inquired whether she was feeling all right, she launched into a story about an incident that had taken place at the local community college with another program resident, Leslie, earlier that day. She presented the sequence of events in the following narrative:

> [She] went and told our teacher at school that we live in a home for prostitutes. A few of us go to the same class every day and see these same people. I was pissed when I found out. We are all trying to change and trying to lose that word, "hoes." You know, I'm not a ho anymore. I'm trying to better myself. So when I found out I told her to shut her mouth and don't speak about me that way.

Hilda's story illustrates how clients engaged in mutual monitoring of one another in order to sustain newly formed, tenuous roles and identities.

Shawnta's statement similarly emphasizes the importance of mutual monitoring among clients in order to retain alternative roles and identities:

> We tell each other that we represent Phoenix when we go out in public because once we get outside [of the house] we want to let our hair down but we have to tell ourselves before we get out of the van, you are what you represent. By reminding myself to remember who I am now and what I represent gives me the willpower to keep a straight eye towards my destination and not worry about the traffic or what's going on all around me.

Another normative control mechanism, affective bonds, undergirded both mutual monitoring and role modeling. Affection for other clients and the development of interpersonal relationships motivated certain women to serve as role models to less advanced residents. These bonds fueled enactments of mutual monitoring among clients, premised on emotional investment in another's successful transition out of sex work and into a conventional lifestyle. When these informal controls were a pervasive feature of a PSO's culture, and thereby provided some regulation of members' talk and behavior, it was more challenging for women to resist normative prescriptions because they were accountable to others.

Melissa, a 42-year-old white woman, worked full-time at a local movie theater where she recently had been promoted to the position of assistant manager. She was also enrolled in classes at the local community college, studying business. She loved her job and claimed to enjoy "earning money the responsible way." In fact, she aspired to become the head manager of the theater one day and believed her business classes would help her attain this position.

As I drove her to work one weekday, I asked her what she liked best about the program. Melissa said that the support she received from other residents was integral to her recovery, and by their example she was inspired to change her life. As one of the most advanced residents, she believed it was her job to likewise monitor and mentor the other clients—encourage them but also point out when they committed talk and behaviors that undermined their transformation. Melissa's statement illustrated how normative controls (mutual monitoring, affective ties, and mentorship) operated between residents:

> The ladies that came before me in the program supported me and gave me the inspiration to want to do certain things for myself and be different. When I first came in they were where I am at today. And knowing it could be done by seeing them do it was important to me. I talk to them. I show them what I built up by allowing myself to trust other people in the program. If you don't build up trust with the other women and staff, this is where you are going to be [motions with her hands close to the ground], whereas if you build up trust you can be standing at this point instead [motions to above her head]. It helps to look to the residents who came before me because they were in the same place I was and now I can see them doing amazing things with their lives.

Shawnta, like Melissa, regularly felt compelled to offer advice and corrections to the newer residents. She declared: "I take it upon myself to try to explain things to some of the younger clients—I take on a mother role, I guess by trying to tell her what to do, what not to do. But some women take it as criticism instead of me trying to help them." I asked her if any of the residents appreciate this guidance, to which she nodded and explained:

Oh, yes. I've helped Evie [two months into the program] and she realizes the help and she thanks me for it. She is appreciative. And the criticism that I give her she accepts it and she learns from it and she tries. I have to commend her on that—she tries. If she can't cook, she will ask me: "Can I watch you today when you cook a certain meal?" And that just shows me that she is willing. And if she's willing, then I'm willing too. I love you for even trying. I told her this morning she gets an "A" for effort. So don't trip. She asked me where does this bowl go instead of leaving it there. She wanted to know where it went. You don't have to put it up, just tell me where it goes. I told her that will enable her to know where everything goes in the kitchen and before you know it, you will have the routine down. This goes with changing her old behaviors and her life. That's the way it was for me and she is very willing. She accepts when she makes mistakes, she'll go back and do them. She may not want to but she does it gracefully.

Sally, Phoenix's residential director, also highlighted the importance of peer role models, mutual monitoring, and the formation of affective bonds, particularly for the less advanced clients:

We call the older residents the mainstay . . . they are the ones who know how to do it. They can model—it's kind of the oldest child kind of thing. When there aren't many role models, it is a lot more work on the part of staff in terms of directing behaviors and modifying their behaviors and offering checks and balances for decision making and that kind of stuff. So it makes a big difference when you don't have a senior resident around.

Informal methods of control were rarely enacted among the clients at the remaining two programs, Safe Place and Seeds. On occasion a few members attempted to practice them; however, because they were not normative within the organizational culture, these efforts were largely ineffective in producing the desired alterations. For example, I observed Olivia, an advanced Safe Place client, perform mutual monitoring among her peers based on her interest in their well-being. As one of the oldest residents, she took it upon herself to chastise women when she felt they were not taking the program seriously (i.e., not amending their talk and behavior). I asked her to elaborate how she went about this:

> You know, I try to tell them why I would really like to be off drugs [and out of prostitution] for real . . . I'll point out what they are doing and the types of old behavior they do that end up hurting them. Because we all have something in common and I'm not the youngest here, I'm 51 years old. I'm not ashamed to speak my mind or use some of the situations I've experienced in my past to help others better themselves.

Yet Olivia's attempts to enforce normative controls onto others were generally ignored by them. Essentially, the absence of formal and informal control mechanisms at Safe Place and Seeds resulted in organizational cultures where there was minimal impetus to adopt a different role and identity.

Resisting Role and Identity Change

Throughout this chapter, I contend that organizational cultures with pervasive control mechanisms facilitate client embracement of a new role and identity. Conversely, the environments where these forces are absent tend to constrain such changes. Temporality is another factor that helps us understand whether clients experience this transformation. The longer a woman remains in a program, the greater her exposure to intensive socialization that champions substantial lifestyle shifts, making it more likely she will follow suit. In regards to the static clients, my study unearths the following patterns: Clients who did not indicate signs of role and identity change had been in a PSO for a relatively short period of time (almost always three months or less), and were usually affiliated with a program that sustained very few, if any, control mechanisms.

The dimensions of time relevant to a program operated at two levels—organizational and individual. PSOs established the maximum length of time clients could remain in the program, and women decided how long they persisted within those parameters. Safe Place and Seeds had relatively short program durations for clients (three months and two weeks, respectively) compared to New Horizons and Phoenix (two years each). Thus women within the shorter programs were not only subjected to few social control mechanisms, but they also had a fairly brief window of time to experience role and identity changes. The residents who continually resisted alternations at long-term PSOs would eventually either voluntarily leave the program or be so disruptive and unruly that the PSO ejected them. The cases of attrition reflect a weeding out process of unyielding clients over time, and those who remain end up embracing a different role and identity.

Carla, a white 21-year-old, had been at Safe Place for approximately six weeks. She was a self-proclaimed tomboy whose wardrobe confirmed this description, as she regularly wore baseball caps, oversized jeans, baggy T-shirts with slogans, and high-top tennis shoes. Carla was known for her extremely volatile personality, manifested in her hostile and aggressive interactions with other clients and staff members. Staff and other residents noted her frequent absences at required group classes, and when in attendance she disrupted the activities with little consequence. The topic of one session focused on the pitfalls of addiction, especially as they related to prostitution, and the women watched a film on drug addiction followed by a group discussion. After the film ended, Carla stood up and loudly remarked to the group that she could not believe the main character had refused to accept pills from a drug dealer. She exclaimed: "I would have done it! It's free man!" A few of the other clients glanced at one another and rolled their eyes in response. The attending staff member ignored her comments and instead called on other residents to solicit their reactions to the film.

This was not an isolated incident, but rather comprised a general pattern of talk and behavior that implied a resistance to role and identity changes. On a different occasion, during a break in between classes the women gathered on the outside patio and decided to play a game of charades to let off some steam. One skit was to act as a married couple that was having trouble controlling their children. Carla volunteered to be the husband in the skit. Another staff member and I were in the background watching the game. Carla strutted around, barking commands at her "wife," and another resident interjected, "Show some emotion," to which Carla gleefully replied, "I'm high, so I can't." Of course, Carla was not actually on drugs, but she chose to incorporate it into the skit. She next donned the role of pimp, as she instructed her "wife" to "get out there and work, bitch!" The implications of her performance were clear: The woman should earn money from prostitution and return it to her pimp. These instances of play were all too familiar, as they underscored Carla's ongoing attachment to prostitution and its surrounding subculture.

A week or so later, I observed Carla in an altercation with another client. A group of residents, a staff member, and I sat on a picnic table on the porch when Carla walked by and commanded one client to come inside so she could talk with her. The woman refused, and Carla stood at a nearby table staring at the woman in an obvious attempt at intimidation. Moments later she yelled, "Fuck you," and pounded her fist on the table to elicit some response. The recipient of this attack remained silently in her seat with a defiant expression on her face. To my surprise, the staff member ignored this outburst and Carla stalked into the house cursing profusely.

Sandra provides another illustration of client repudiation of an alternative role and identity. She was an African American woman in her thirties who had been at Safe Place for close to one month when she openly shared her doubts about leaving prostitution. Sandra expressed her ambivalence about sobriety in particular, and given the interconnectedness of substance abuse and sex work, the following statement belied any transformation: "Being sober seems boring and I do not see the point in it or benefits gained from it. I'll try to stay sober but may use drugs again. When I leave I'll probably return to what I was doing before."

Jamie, a white Seeds client, regularly isolated herself from the staff and other women in the program for the duration of the two-week program. She begrudgingly attended group classes but remained silent, and boldly refused to participate in any of the class activities. During a lunch break, I approached her and asked why she was so quiet. Jamie stated: "The staff and other clients don't communicate with me and I don't with them. I stay to myself because I don't really relate to the program." I inquired whether she felt she had changed since arriving at the program, to which she responded:

> No, I still feel the same, I haven't changed. The only change is that I'm not walking the streets at this moment because I'm in here. I feel bad about myself that I'm not out there on the streets, where I feel good because guys give me a lot of attention. Once I leave the program I will go back to being a prostitute, just to live.

Before and after the class each day, other clients observed Jamie accompanied by her "boyfriend," a notorious local pimp. Her statements, coupled with this behavior, provide evidence that she continued to occupy the deviant, criminal role associated with street prostitution.

Demonstrations of client recalcitrance were typical among the women at Seeds and Safe Place for the reasons previously discussed. But there were a few novice residents at the long-term PSOs who also refused to alter their identity and role, such as Susanna. It was clear that Susanna, who is white, still identified as a prostitute and maintained that role via her talk and behavior. After a brief stint at New Horizons earlier in the year, where she returned to the streets for a few months, she was readmitted to the program after the CEO tracked her down and pleaded with her to come back. When I was first introduced to her, she had been in the program just shy of two months. I asked about her reintegration and she verbally expressed an unwillingness to amend her talk or behavior:

I call what they do here brainwashing. They try to teach me responsibility
and more self-respect but I still don't have it because I haven't changed the
mental me. I usually get to a point and say, "Fuck it, it's over. I don't care.
I don't care if George Bush is looking for me. I need to get out of here!"

Susanna's actions likewise preserved this role and identity. She avoided
interactions with other residents whenever possible and used her part-time
job at the program to justify her absences from required classes. The temporary job consisted of cleaning the staff offices to earn extra cash, osten-
sibly to help support her daughter, while the regular cleaning lady was ill.

As she was cleaning the offices one morning while the staff members
were in a meeting, she sat down at an empty desk next to me and made
a phone call. I overheard her discussing her boyfriend, who had been
arrested for possession of drugs and was currently serving time in jail.
In a low voice, she told the person she needed to get some drugs and
had no money, but was "willing to do what it takes to get some." Another
staff member, who returned to her desk during this conversation, also
noted the content. Susanna quickly terminated the call and immediately vacated the office. The staff member turned to me, remarked that
Susanna was up to "no good," and stated she planned to report her to the
program director. She vented: "How is she ever going to change, talking
and acting like that? She sounded like she was trying to get drugs from
somebody. She wouldn't act like that if higher up staff were present. That's
a bad sign that she is up to her old ways. I don't think she's going to last
around here for long." New Horizons staff and other residents doubted
Susanna's ability to remain out of prostitution for long, and most program clients shunned her. Upon learning about the phone exchange, the
director asked Susanna to leave the program immediately. The fact that
she was still a neophyte at New Horizons (and maintained distance from
other residents) provides insight into her untoward talk and behavior.

Social control mechanisms *and* time spent in a PSO are important
considerations when assessing whether clients move into this final
phase of exiting. These factors encompass meso-level phenomena (e.g.,

organizational practices, group socialization, affective ties) as well as individual agency (e.g., making decisions about remaining in the program, behavioral choices). The two PSOs that I categorize as short-term maintained structures and cultures that hindered clients' construction and implementation of a conventional role and sense of self.

The accounts of clients, both compliant and resistant, draw attention to another feature vital to role exits—commitment. Commitment to an alternative role, identity, and lifestyle is fostered at the organizational and individual levels. PSOs can amplify a woman's dedication to these transformations by instituting commitment-building mechanisms, which in turn become normative practices among residents. And a client can demonstrate her resolution by exhibiting various behavioral markers of change.

Commitment-Building Mechanisms

Particular PSO cultures uphold commitment-building mechanisms, which are organizationally based strategies intended to strengthen client dedication to a new role and identity. Researchers unearth that these mechanisms operate across a variety of groups and contexts, including social movements and utopian communes.[22] In her study of utopian communes, organizational scholar Rosabeth Kanter argues that the most successful and long-standing are those that developed numerous commitment-building tactics because they deepen member loyalty.[23] When present within PSOs, these tactics emerge in the form of client cultural and social isolation, transformation, and public confession.

Throughout chapters 4 and 5, I discuss how long-term residential PSOs sequester clients from street subcultures (and affiliates) for substantial periods of time, which often facilitates distance from prostitution and an embracement of a nondeviant sense of self and role. Isolation often enriches one's commitment because it produces affective bonds between residents and those who emulate prosocial talk and behavior (e.g., staff members, advanced residents) that in turn increase personal accountability. I refer to this practice as a coercive mechanism of control, which can simultaneously strengthen a woman's commitment to implement significant lifestyle changes.

The prioritization of client transformations at the organizational level also constitutes a commitment-building strategy. Recall that New Horizons and Phoenix were sites where this transformation served as an organizational goal, and staff members worked hard to bring it to fruition. Earlier in this chapter I provided examples from the staff that underscore the degree to which they value conversion-like experiences among clients, stemming from the belief that they are paramount for women to effectively leave prostitution. Accordingly, transformation became a normative practice where most residents eventually displayed high commitment to implement and sustain such changes. Alternatively, the other two PSOs and their staff members did not harbor similar expectations for clients, which ultimately diminished their dedication to embrace another role and identity.

The final type of commitment-building mechanism, also established at the organizational level, included client public confession. Phoenix was the only site where I observed this mechanism. The director, Sally, strongly encouraged residents to attend local public speaking events and discuss their experiences as street prostitutes. Most events were fundraisers for the program, public health seminars, or community educational seminars. During my fieldwork at Phoenix, a few clients carried out this task. The very nature of public confession, also known as witnessing, was for a woman to contrast her life in sex work to her life postprostitution. In these speeches, clients typically discussed the deleterious effects of working in prostitution as well as the changes they had made since enrolling in Phoenix. This public act highlighted her commitment to shed her former self and adopt a conventional, law-abiding role and identity. Additionally, the practice of witnessing helped clients to cognitively, emotionally, and physically maintain these alterations.

The program director, Sally, was regularly invited to speak at community events and therefore encouraged Phoenix residents to partake in the presentation. Shawnta, 45 years old, had been at the program for almost eight months when she gave her first public talk at a local high school about her experiences with drug addiction and prostitution. After witnessing, Shawnta was elated by the overall experience. She felt that this was her way to give back to the community and prepare for her future career as a counselor. She summarized her experience and what it did for her:

> I want to learn to be a productive person and be able to live in a community where I am contributing to the well-being of society. I want to do something positive in my life. I want to be able to hold my head up and not worry about doing demoralizing things in order to survive. I want to live, not just survive or exist. And these talks help me because my goal is to become a counselor. I would love to be an HIV peer counselor or treatment advocate so that I can help to educate young people by doing some speaking engagements—go to colleges and schools and speak to people about my life story. How it was and where I am at today. Give them some sort of inspiration.

Indeed, Shawnta's comments imply she found public confession cathartic, as this performance offered her a way to actively participate in and contribute to conventional society. Ultimately, witnessing fortified her devotion to this burgeoning role and identity.

Assessing Individual Commitment to a New Role and Identity

While certain PSOs attempt to increase client dedication to a different lifestyle, role, and identity through their implementation of commitment-building mechanisms, commitment is also contingent upon the individual. Indeed, personal commitment is another consideration that affects whether a woman moves through the phases of role exiting or not. For instance, even in long-term residential PSOs where clients are subjected to omnipresent forces of controls that usually engender changes, there are still those who are unyielding. Such recalcitrance can be attributed to a lack of time in the program, as I assert earlier in the chapter, or can result from a low commitment. The women who progress through these three phases tend to be highly committed to leave sex work.

Much of this manuscript focuses on the ways in which PSOs and their staff members constrain or facilitate the role-exiting phases among clients. When it comes to the construction and adoption of an alternative self and role, programs are especially relevant because they can provide the blueprint for what each entails. To that end, sociologist Ross Haenfler argues that social actors create personal identities and action repertoires based upon guidelines and structure provided by a "community of meaning."[24] PSO staff members and clients cultivate this community of meaning together, manifested in the organizational culture. Although clients have agency to formulate their new roles and identities, their designs are often profoundly affected by the cultural contexts in which they are immersed, which promote particular values, mores, and codes of conduct. Moreover, various control mechanisms—both formal and informal—shape this process of change. The degree to which clients emulate these ideal traits as they transition demonstrates their commitment to radically amend their lifestyle.

Consider Derica, who displayed a strong commitment to leave sex work and become a different person. She stressed how New Horizons helped boost her self-esteem and self-worth, internal alterations that heightened her resolve to exit:

> You know, going through New Horizons gave me a sense of worth and made me feel like a human being. I didn't feel that way before when I was working on the streets. And a big part of that is the commitment to changing. Do you want to be committed to doing life the way it should be done or do you want to be committed to killing yourself on a daily basis? You gotta want to change. You can say it out of your mouth but you got to want to change, deep down inside.

Ma S. also emphasized the importance of clients' dedication to exit prostitution and transform their lives because it impacts their success. She explained:

> In order to make it in this program, you can't come because someone else wants you to be here. In order to make it, you have to want to be able to

find your inner self and not turn tricks and not do drugs. You need to be here for yourself. You need to be willing to become different.

In spite of her hopes for these women, she felt there was only so much she and the other staff members could do to bring about such changes if clients lacked determination and commitment.

Commitment is the foundation that undergirds a woman's construction and embracement of a different role and identity. In his examination of individuals who took on a straight-edge identity, Haenfler ascertains that *essential, secondary,* and *peripheral* behaviors bolster this transition.[25] These behavioral indices, coupled with verbal cues, illuminate PSO client commitment to lifestyle transformations post prostitution.

Essential Behaviors

Essential client behaviors that indicate a dedication to change include maintaining sobriety and avoidance of sex work. Such behaviors are prerequisite characteristics that suggest a minimal commitment to uphold the newly formed sense of self and social position. Recall Hayley's story described earlier in the chapter. In the following statement, she contrasts her former self with her current self, sustained through her newly embraced role, both of which are removed from sex work and substance abuse:

> Right now I respect myself and love myself. I love working—I'm a part-time loan officer, a part-time nanny and a part-time real estate assistant—and like what I'm doing. I'm ashamed for what I've done in the past but I can't change the past. I can only look at the future. I can focus on keeping clean and sober, working my jobs, being involved at my church . . . All I can say is that I don't ever want to go back—to the person I used to be.

Veronica, an African American Safe Place graduate—and one of the few who indicated a role and identity transformation at that site—underscored her commitment to these alterations by abstaining from drugs and eschewing prostitution. It was evident she felt her current role and identity were far more respectable now that she no longer engaged in sex work or drug use: "I used to think of myself as an old crackhead: I would fuck for crack and money. But now I don't and won't. I put that behind me. I see myself as a better person, no longer a prostitute or crackhead. I've changed my mind as I've changed my baggage."

Hilda entered prostitution at the age of twenty-four. Although she only stayed in the trade for five years, a relatively short tenure compared to many other clients, she claimed to feel much guilt about her actions and knew it was wrong. She took it upon herself to find Phoenix and enroll because in spite of wanting to change, Hilda recognized that she needed help to maintain sobriety in order to leave prostitution. She confided:

> I lost all track of how to live out there, using drugs and prostituting. There are things I want out of life that I've always wanted out of life. I knew, even then, that if I continued to live like that I wasn't going to better myself. I could have stayed at home to try to get clean but I knew that wouldn't work . . . too much freedom and temptation there. I just needed some stability in my life and I felt Phoenix could provide it. So, in order to get the things I want in life, I am fully committed to doing the work.

I asked her why she believed Phoenix could help her implement such changes, and she responded, "Because of the success rate. How long it's been in the business. And from the things that other girls had told me about the place . . . I just knew they could." Hilda upheld this commitment as she remained sober and out of prostitution for the nine months she had been in the program.

The above accounts emphasize that sobriety was an essential behavior, and one that was necessary to maintain any sort of commitment to a lifestyle transition. Social scientists Linda Cusick and Matthew Hickman claim that drug use and street prostitution are interdependent, thereby making it extremely challenging to desist without sobriety.[26] Maintaining sobriety was certainly a challenge for clients, but so was drastically amending their long-standing sexual practices. American women are instructed to be sexually alluring and available yet not promiscuous, which constitute contradictory behaviors.[27] Deciphering what comprises appropriate sexual behaviors may be particularly challenging for women whose livelihood depended on their overt sexual availability for purchase for good portions of their lives.

Feminist sociologist Patricia Hill Collins argues that the cult of true womanhood still abounds today, setting the precedence that women should possess four virtues: piety, purity, submissiveness and domesticity.[28] In an analysis of female street prostitutes, historian Judith Walkowitz explores their castigation by Victorian era middle-class individuals, especially women, for their breach of female respectability.[29] Prostitutes defy conventional gender expectations through their dress, sexual conduct, manners, and crude language. Many of the same prized markers of femininity continue to persist today, and women who do not adhere to these guidelines are subjected to societal judgment and even condemnation.

For female prostitutes, another essential behavior that intimates a commitment to a prosocial, nondeviant self and role is a fundamental reorientation to sex acts, where they occur within monogamous relationships and without compensation. New Horizons and Phoenix supported policies of abstinence for clients for the duration of their time in the program, predicated on the belief that clients need to adopt a different approach to sex and intimate relationships with men. Rayna, the chief operating officer at New Horizons, articulated their stance on client sexuality:

> It's important for clients to remain celibate for the two years that they're here because they never knew their selves as anything that wasn't sexual. I think that to become anything or anyone else they need to understand that their body is a temple and a gift, and that they shouldn't buy and sell it. In order to do so, you have to take sex out of the equation for a while.

At Phoenix, I observed residents warn one another to be aware of their tendencies to use sexuality to their gain, especially when interacting with men. In the following example, a resident expressed her desire to select a male Alcoholics Anonymous (AA) sponsor, and other members quickly pointed out the hazards in doing so. One outspoken resident voiced that they must all be cautious of reproducing entrenched negative male-female behavioral patterns, summarized in the following statement:

> I think you should have a female sponsor and I'll tell you why. I wanted to get a male sponsor before and I thank God I didn't. I talked to other members to get their input and I could see that I was attracted to him both sexually and because he knew the program. I thank God that I didn't do anything with him. I realize now that I had ulterior motives because sex is the only way I knew how to relate to men and get something from them.

Beverly, a resident of New Horizons, also declared her intent to remain celibate for some time:

> Everybody doesn't deserve that gift. It would be nice to have a companion, a soul mate, but fix yourself first, and everything else will fall in place. That old mindset was what allowed me to sleep with anyone without thinking twice. I don't want to do that to myself anymore because my body is a temple.

Her chaste behaviors aligned with this verbal proclamation, and together they implied an essential commitment to role and identity transformation. While many women focused on developing an alternative sense of self via sobriety and adjusting their sexual practices, some were also acutely concerned with their social identity, or how others perceived them.

Melissa, who had resided at Phoenix for 18 months, found that as she redefined her personal identity, upheld via essential verbal and behavioral changes, outsiders began to view and treat her differently as well. She was elated by this recent shift in social identity:

> I like the respectable way I look. I get a better response from people. I could always count on a man's response before but now a woman will say

hello to me on the streets. Before they would turn their heads the other way because they felt like I was being disrespectful with the outfit I had on and what I was doing out there [knowing I was a prostitute].

Conversely, women who did not maintain sobriety or were unwilling to adjust their sexual orientation to men demonstrated little commitment to transition out of sex work. When I asked Lily whether she was committed to leaving prostitution, she candidly replied: "I dunno, sometimes I really miss being out there. I'm not really friends with anyone here and I am bored most of the time. I don't think I changed so far." Lily, in fact, lamented the fact that she was currently out of the trade: "I feel bad about myself because I'm not out there on the street, getting that validation." Although still sober, Lily's comments suggest that both her role and identity remained intricately connected to the act of selling sex.

By the end of the two-week program, Jessica, a white Seeds client, displayed no commitment to change her role and identity. Her statement was unequivocal: "Yeah, I'm always going to be a ho! I ain't never going to change." Similarly, Susanna did not engage in essential behaviors or talk either, as she had already left the program once to return to prostitution and drug use, and was caught trying to score upon her reenrollment. During a one-on-one conversation about her progress, she frankly told me: "I'm not gonna say [I'm] so much committed to change because I'm gonna be honest: If I can get high and make money off prostituting for the rest of my life I probably would because it's easy money."

Secondary Behaviors

When clients engaged in secondary behaviors, they indicated a greater level of commitment to the adoption of a transformed role and identity. Such behaviors, coupled with verbal signals, included educational attainment, securing legal employment, sustaining social support networks, and reestablishing relationships with their children. Felicia engaged in a myriad of both essential and secondary behaviors as she focused on her sobriety, educational attainment, and her career. She highlighted these accomplishments during our interview:

> You know, I'm really a beautiful person and my life is really precious to me. I now make healthier decisions than I've *ever* made. Even before I became addicted to drugs, I wasn't making the healthiest decisions as I'm making today. Since being in the program I went back to school, got my associate's degree, and am working on my bachelor's degree with a focus on social service programs, which serve incarcerated mothers. My life did a 180-degree turn.

Derica also held a steady job, and maintained her support network with program staff members and residents after graduation. She recalled:

> I first started working at a diner when I had been at New Horizons for about a year. That was the beginning of getting me back into the workforce. It helped me to be able to do what I do today, which is to work with the developmentally disabled. I always enjoyed working with the mentally disabled. My field has always been social services. I like helping people. Within 10 months, I got a promotion and became a supervisor.

Her ongoing interactions with social support networks undergirded her commitment to this new role and identity:

> I have a lot of people that I can call when things are getting overwhelming for me. Not only my family but also New Horizons staff members, and older residents, program graduates. I'm in a Prostitutes Anonymous program that I go to regularly. By all means necessary, I go to those meetings. I've been through counseling. So I seek out help and have a lot of support nowadays.

New Horizons staff members also emphasized that these markers of commitment—careers, sobriety, housing—are integral to uphold role and identity alternations. Mark, the chief development officer, proclaimed:

This program helps sustain sobriety, get them off the streets, get them into stable housing, get them into some sort of job or career path that will keep them away from [prostitution] and being homeless. We are trying to show them that their life has dignity, that their life has worth, that they are beautiful people, that they should expect things from life. They can take control of their lives. They can do positive things. If anything I think we show these women that they are not prostitutes, that they may have been prostituting, but they are not prostitutes. They can and should envision themselves as something else—as a woman who has rights and value.

Another secondary behavior that enriched commitment to a new sense of self revolved around motherhood and repairing damaged relationships with children. Such findings are consistent with prior desistance research that illustrates female offenders cite children as catalysts for the changes they make.[30] A majority of the women in this study had children (about 75 percent), but most had lost custody or were estranged from them during their tenure in sex work. As a result, mending these relationships was paramount for many PSO clients, and fulfilling the duties of a mother showed a strong devotion to a transformed lifestyle. Derica, for instance, had two adult daughters and lamented the fact that she was not around to raise them. Although her relationship with her eldest daughter was still tenuous, she perceived an improvement in their rapport after she enrolled in New Horizons and embraced change:

I used to resent the fact that I wasn't the mother to my daughter that she is to her children. After dealing with some of my baggage while in the program, my daughter and I have a real close bond. She saw that I was working on me and that I wanted a relationship with her—I wanted to be her mother again—and the relationship got much better.

Melissa relinquished custody of her two sons when they were seven and five, due to a severe drug addiction, her engagement in prostitution, and following a separation from her husband. Since that time she had intermittent communication with her youngest son via telephone calls every year or two, but had no contact with her oldest since she lost custody. After cultivating a different identity and role while at Phoenix, Melissa expended considerable effort to reestablish relationships with them, denoting a commitment to this new lifestyle. She described a litany of essential and secondary behaviors she performed:

> I talk to my sons now. Now that I've got my life together they want to find out who their real mother is . . . They want to get to know me. But I could never have did that if I was still out there using. If I was using, I would still be in the life of prostitution. Today, I finished going to school. I have been working at a job for almost a year now. I am in contact with my children and in contact with my brother and my half-sister. Today, I have healthy relationships with people. My goal is number one to stay clean and sober. My second goal would be to maintain the same job I'm at or a better job. To keep my apartment, buy me a car, and to be able to start visiting my sons or having them come out and visit me. So both of my children are very excited to actually have a chance to meet me and I want them to meet me and get to know me so we can spend that time together.

Amanda, a program graduate, was the mother of three girls who were now adults. After her husband (their father) died from AIDS, she began using drugs and engaged in prostitution at the late age of forty. She recalled the shame her daughters felt when they observed her at work on the streets: "My daughters would pass me by and wouldn't stop. The two oldest ones would holler at me. They were so ashamed of me. I really feel that now." The relationships deteriorated and she had little communication with her daughters. Amanda reported that they had much healthier relationships now, which helped her maintain her transformed role and identity. Through this routine contact with her girls she was able to act as a mother again, even though they were in their twenties. Her middle daughter was currently incarcerated, so Amanda had volunteered to raise her grandchild during the interim and continued to mother her to make up for lost time:

I visit her and keep in touch and am there for her no matter what. This is my daughter so I'm going to be there no matter what. I wasn't able to before [while in prostitution] but I can now. It's her second time around in jail and I'm hoping that since I've changed my life—she's so proud of me and talks so very good of me in there—that she will jump on the wagon herself.

Some PSO staff members also believed that reunification between women and their children was extremely beneficial to their long-term success. As the New Horizons CEO remarked: "If they can reunify in any way with their children and become a parent again they are successful, and we encourage that. If you are a mother and don't reconnect with your child it will break your heart and prevent you from healing."

Peripheral Behaviors

When clients engage in peripheral behaviors they demonstrate exceptionally high levels of commitment to a new role and identity. These behaviors are uncommon among PSO clients because they require considerable time and energy to fulfill. They occur when clients work in professions that specifically help drug addicts and prostitutes, continue to volunteer at PSOs after graduation, or follow a spiritual calling.

After graduating from New Horizons, Felicia began volunteering weekly at a program situated within the county jail intended for incarcerated women so that she could give back to the community. She drew on her past experiences and attempted to relate to these women based on her prior involvement with the criminal justice system and prostitution. Recognizing that many others also engaged in sex work, Felicia felt that sharing her story of transformation could help elicit hope among them and a desire to alter their behavior.

Sherita also volunteered time at New Horizons when she was near graduation, even though she was concurrently working a full-time job and in the process of moving out. She took mentoring seriously and spent most of this time supporting and speaking with the current residents. The program staff was so impressed by her dedication that they eventually offered her a part-time position as an outreach worker for the program upon her graduation. To that end, she regularly visited local jails, disseminated information about New Horizons to incarcerated women, relayed her story of leaving the trade, and encouraged them to follow suit by enrolling in the program.

The first job Beverly obtained while in the program was working at a Hilton Hotel as a receptionist. Yet every evening after work, she still returned to New Horizons to spend time with the staff and other residents. I asked her why she did this, and she replied, "You know I just always came back and tried to give back to the women that I left behind and the women that then came behind them . . . I just want to give back, support them, and show that it [the program] works." Beverly felt compelled to contribute to New Horizons because the program had given her so much, but her daily presence and mentoring far exceeded that of other program graduates and volunteers.

Rochelle, who worked as a legal assistant part-time, also wanted to do something that would directly benefit prostitutes and drug addicts. In addition to volunteering at Phoenix a few days a week following her graduation, she earned the credentials to become a HIV counselor. She then was employed by Phoenix part-time to run their crisis center, conduct street outreach, and test prostitutes for sexually transmitted diseases (STDs). She described her responsibilities:

> I've exceeded my goals since graduating because who would have known I was gonna be a certified HIV counselor. You know, today I'm grateful to be able to identify with the clients, and I really believe that God put me in this job for a reason and that is to help somebody because I have been there [in prostitution and drug-addiction]. I run the crisis center at night by myself right now, I do a little street outreach at times, I do testing for STDs. I've been certified to do all the testing and of course the pre- and postcounseling that's required.

At New Horizons and Phoenix advanced and newly graduated clients acted as role models to newer clients, and this performance became entrenched within these organizational cultures as normative controls. Upon graduation, however, most women stopped volunteering regularly at these settings as they became preoccupied and busy with their own lives. Some individuals—Felicia, Sherita, Beverly, and Rochelle—continued to regularly volunteer at a PSO and occupied jobs that entailed working with similar populations.

The final peripheral behavior is when clients display an extraordinary dedication to their religious beliefs by selecting a career path that centers on their spiritual beliefs, one that would also encompass a rigid lifestyle removed from the elements associated with sex work. Indeed, these women desire to serve others based upon their strongly held religious convictions and dedicate their lives to this mission. Marleen was the only PSO client who exhibited these behaviors, which became defining markers of her new role and identity. During my fieldwork observations, she sequestered herself in her room two times each day in order to read the Bible and pray, wrote letters to nuns at a local convent and asked them to visit her, and attended the voluntary on-site Bible study every Wednesday. She invited me and other program residents to pray with her and read the Bible. Marleen believed that God delivered her from drug addiction and prostitution so that she could do something more meaningful with her life, namely, to serve God. As she neared graduation from Safe Place, she planned to do mission work for the church and proselytize. She explained:

I used to call myself an outlaw because that's how I thought of myself. This program has helped me look at myself differently, you know. I now have choices. I know I'm worth something and it was a big thing just realizing that I have choices and that I'm worth making those right choices now. I'm totally committed to this new me because I'm totally committed to what God wants for me. He has much greater plans for me, and I need to comply with them. I plan to do mission work with the church when I am done here. God was really helpful by showing me I don't need to do that stuff [prostitution, drugs] anymore. I know that I'll never return to active addiction or prostitution again now that I know my calling.

In fact, right before exiting the field, I found out that Marleen applied to a convent to become a nun.

Certain PSO clients exhibit talk and behavior to denote distance from prostitution as well as their embracement of an alternative role and identity. Yet an individual's commitment to such changes is central to this process. I find that essential, secondary, and peripheral behaviors, coupled with aligned talk, incrementally imply greater commitment to a conventional role and identity among PSO clients.

To Change or Not, That Is the Question

After women enter a PSO and establish distance from sex work, they finally begin to talk and behave in ways that indicate an adoption of a different role and identity. A component of sociologist Helen Rose Ebaugh's role-exiting theory dovetails with this latter phase, which she refers to as creating an "ex-role," where the individual makes life-encompassing changes to her role, identity, behaviors, and lifestyle.[31] Yet Ebaugh's theory does not consider any external forces that affect these alterations. In this chapter, I unearth particular organizational characteristics and practices that either promote or impede PSO clients' identity and role transformations.

First, PSOs with entrenched coercive control mechanisms strongly encourage role distancing and the embracement of a new role and identity among clients. These organizational mechanisms include program structure, policies, discipline and rewards, and demarcated goals. Second, settings where informal controls are normative among clients subsequently subject them to intense socialization processes. They are evident in the formation of affective bonds, mutual monitoring, and role models, all of which champion client alterations. Sociologists Peter Berger and Thomas Luckmann consider secondary socialization to be exceedingly paramount as individuals acquire new identities and construct their reality.[32] Third, certain PSOs also implement commitment-building mechanisms (client isolation, transformations as organizational goals, and public confession) in order to bolster individual dedication to embrace and uphold a conventional role and identity.

Of the four PSOs, New Horizons and Phoenix most closely resembled total institutions due to their structure, rules, and constant staff supervision of clients. However, these PSOs were arguably not quite as extreme, given that women were not imprisoned or physically prevented from leaving if they so desired. Moreover, as clients advanced in the programs they incrementally acquired additional physical freedom and autonomy to leave the premises in order to attend educational classes, 12-step meetings, and eventually part-time work. As a result of this organizational model and the accompanying forces of control, I conclude that most women at New Horizons and Phoenix move through the role-exiting phases and ultimately adopt a newfound sense of self and role. Those who remain stagnant eventually fall out of the program.

In comparison, client role and identity transformations were uncommon for those immersed within Safe Place and Seeds. Formal and informal control mechanisms were either absent or ineffective at these sites, and the short program durations for the women limited their exposure to what few forces of control existed. Altogether, these conditions engendered organizational cultures where there were few external pressures on clients to change.

As previously discussed, even New Horizons and Phoenix, programs steeped in social control mechanisms, were not able to always cultivate client transformations due to individual agency. One explanation for client recalcitrance can be attributed to a woman's motivations for leaving the trade and the salience of these reasons, which I explored in chapter 2. Another consideration is a woman's lack of personal commitment to implement a radically different lifestyle, replete with a revamped identity and role. Clients displayed the extent of their commitment through their talk and performance of essential, secondary, and peripheral behaviors. Past research asserts that identity and role changes are unlikely if there is a lack of commitment to them.[33] And sociologists Doug McAdam and Ronnelle Paulsen posit that individual commitment to a particular identity can always be enhanced through one's organizational ties.[34]

6

Getting Out

Remaining Out of Sex Work

When I first began my fieldwork at Phoenix, Melissa was one of the most advanced program residents. She was often absent from the home due to her full-time job and college classes. But when there she made her presence known by checking in with other residents, serving as a role model, and spending time strategizing with staff about the future and her impending move. Nearing graduation, she considered herself a different person than when she first entered:

> I have built a new foundation to stand on. I am able to go on with my life, have my own apartment soon, and hold down a job. I can establish between right and wrong today. I am independent without doing any illegal things. I also have much higher self-esteem and confidence in myself. I learned that I could do this [life] on my own. So I have no problem believing that Phoenix did me 100 percent good. I'm a very different person now and I never used to think about my future but only thought about what I needed to do immediately. Now I look ahead in my life, with dreams and goals.

Melissa smiled when she recited her accomplishments since enrolling in the program and viewed them as central to her successful transition out of prostitution:

> I finished going to school, earned my GED, and now am taking business college classes. I think the schooling is the most important thing to be

successful. If a person really wants to change their life and make something of themselves they have the opportunity to go as far as they would like to and they have the program's support. I've been at my job for almost a year now, working as an assistant manager at a movie theater. I like who I am. I feel good that people depend on me.

While there are multiple indicators that Melissa had indeed radically changed her role and identity and desisted from prostitution, her story raises the issue of feasibility: whether other female prostitutes can attain similar markers of success.

Overcoming Obstacles

At the beginning of this book I discussed personal, social, economic, and legal challenges female street prostitutes face, which can hamper their efforts to leave the trade.[1] In spite of these obstacles, countless women indeed venture to quit and some manage to remain out of the lifestyle for prolonged periods of time. The few empirical examinations of this transition shed light on the social-psychological factors that undergird it.[2] Even analogous studies on female offender desistance and role exiting illuminate the cognitive alterations integral to such processes.[3] For example, in their research on female desisters, Giordano and colleagues find that religious transformations and children are catalysts for cognitive changes. Despite such revelations, they also call for greater consideration of context as it shapes this process: "A thorough understanding of either female or male adult desistance likely requires that we theorize a more reciprocal relationship between actor and environment and reserve a central place for agency in the change process."[4] While I, too, find that cognitive shifts are a critical component of desistance, my analysis additionally highlights the substantial impact organizations, their members, and external forces have on this transition that subsequently makes it harder for women to recidivate.

To that end, this book generates a model of leaving prostitution that considers the interplay between organizations and individuals, a dynamic that can expedite three central phases inherent to the exiting process: initial exit, role distancing, and embracement of a new role and identity. For each of these phases, I comparatively examine the impact of PSOs by focusing on coercive, normative, and commitment-building social control mechanisms. Instituted at the organizational level, these include physical separation, provision of resources, rewards and punishments, client conversions, and public witnessing. Upheld via interpersonal inter-actions, normative controls appear in the form of fictive families, affective bonds, peer socialization, role models, and disapproval and shunning. Phoenix and New Horizons were two sites where such forces of control were rife and in turn facilitated exiting among women. Conversely, at Seeds and Safe Place, programs where social controls were largely absent, ineffective, or irregularly performed, very few women exhibited indica-tors of desistance.

Beyond powerful forces of control, the agency of women immersed within such environments concurrently guided their progress. These individualistic factors consisted of personal motivations to quit, time in the program, and commitment levels, which can impede or work in conjunction with control mechanisms. This book underscores the inter-connectedness of meso (e.g., social controls, organizational cultures) and micro theories (symbolic interactionism, role and identity transforma-tions), and how multiple levels of analyses can expand our knowledge of the overall desistance and exiting processes.

Maintaining the New Role and Identity

After women leave the sex trade and adopt a conventional role and iden-tity, do they sustain such changes, and if so, how? The question of the permanency of desistance and role exits is a challenging one for scholars, since it is difficult to provide a concrete assessment without longitudinal data on individuals that spans decades. To further complicate matters, people transition into and out of roles over the course of their entire lives, meaning that they likely experience numerous role exits. When it comes to quitting street-level sex work, certain researchers argue that multiple exits or "yo-yoing" is a common phenomenon.[5]

This was not the case among this sample of prostitutes. A majority of them (60 percent) stated that they had worked continuously in the trade with no earlier exits, while only 32.5 percent made an attempt to leave prior to their enrollment in a PSO, albeit unsuccessfully.[6] The previous exits were temporary reprieves from sex work; some were fueled by arrests and incarcerations, while others resulted from personal motivations based upon pregnancy, sobriety, or relationships with family members. None of the women received institutional or organizational support during their past (and failed) efforts to leave.

It is important to remember that when individuals transition from a deviant, criminal role to a conventional one, they face numerous obstacles. During this transition, prostitutes grapple with the effects of stigma, fractured personal relationships, addiction, shame, criminal records, and moral condemnation. Past studies indicate that individuals who successfully leave a role are able to do so because they create an "ex-role" for themselves.[7] This ex-role encompasses a new lifestyle: identity, social circles, employment, and habits. And certain individuals experience role hangover, where their former role and identity continues to be especially salient in their new lives.[8]

As I argued throughout chapter 5, the development of an ex-role, which I refer to as a conventional (or prosocial) role and corresponding identity, is essential for women to quit prostitution. For those who accomplished this transition role hangover was not particularly salient, as they were eager to forget their involvement in the trade and their history. Once they occupied a new social status, attached to an altered sense of self and role, women employed a variety of techniques to retain this new lifestyle.

While on the streets, an overwhelming majority of prostitutes stated that they relied on drugs to cope with the hardships of the trade, their emotions, and the stigma attached to this work. In short, it was a primary coping mechanism for women and a response to daily worries and tribulations. Upon achieving a lifestyle shift, it was paramount that they develop other strategies to help them weather difficulties and challenges that would inevitability surface, so that they could avoid relapse (and a return to sex work). These techniques included retaining relationships with the PSOs, participating in therapeutic support groups, mentoring others, and taking steps to elevate their human and social capital.

Upholding Relationships with the PSO

PSO graduates stressed that their ongoing relationships with PSO staff members and program aftercare services were invaluable systems of support, bolstering their new lifestyle. In illustration of this point, Felicia, a graduate from New Horizons, provided the following story:

> When I first graduated the program, I felt I was out of that umbrella of safety. I walked past the people on the streets and I could see the mannerisms and the behavior and I knew that they were high and, for a moment I . . . my body . . . I don't know if you understand about the disease of addiction and the cravings but for a second I got a craving in my stomach and it started to flip. I immediately went on the train and went to New Horizons. And I talked with the staff about how that made me feel and what I thought. That therapy was a part of how they taught me to stay clean and stay out of prostitution. Basically, when something like that happens, go someplace safe, talk about it, and let it be done. I still use that strategy to this day.

She added that in preparation to leave the facility, she and the staff created an aftercare plan to keep her from returning to her former role. Felicia discussed her plan: "To continue to stay drug and alcohol free and out of prostitution and to stay in subsidized housing until I finish my education."

Hayley also completed New Horizons a few years back, and claimed that the adjustment after the program ended was difficult. To ease her transition she leaned heavily on the program, attended its aftercare services, and voluntarily committed to day treatment for an extended period of time.

Yeah, I had one of the ladies from New Horizons spend the night at my apartment the first day I got it. I was so used to doing things at the program and abiding by their rules that when I was on my own I felt lost. I didn't know what to do . . . After I left I did aftercare, which was day treatment for four months, where I went from 10 to 2 every day. We had meetings and so on and once I completed that my life became adjustable.

Rochelle, who graduated from Phoenix a little over two years ago, continued to meet with the program staff for guidance, support, and direction. She clarified:

I visit the program probably once a month, once every two months. They like us to meet to see if we are managing our money, managing our bills, keeping sober, and so on. That's what I like about this place. Just because you graduated Phoenix, you haven't graduated "the program." I'm close with all the staff members and feel like I'm still a part of the program. That will go on until I choose to move away from here. And I don't plan on doing that anytime soon.

Melissa, a recent Phoenix graduate, believed that accessibility to staff and their encouragement enabled her to sustain a conventional role and identity:

Knowing that you are able to come back to Sally [the director] at any point and say this is how I feel, or Sally, I need help here. Or I'm in a tight spot, do you have some suggestions? Knowing they are always going to be there for me no matter what—it means a lot. Even if I was to move out of state, I know I could still call her and say, I have this problem I need some advice.

Ultimately, it was graduates' regular visits, phone calls, and interactions with the program and staff members that kept these therapeutic relationships strong. Amanda, a seven-month New Horizons graduate, confirmed: "I keep in touch with the program about three to four times a week. I visit when I can and otherwise I will call them. My Narcotics

Anonymous (NA) sponsor is a woman who now works for the program. And I'll call the girls currently in the program to see how they are doing." Felicia also made routine visits to New Horizons for events and on-site 12-step meetings. When I asked when she last visited, she recalled, "I was just there for Thanksgiving dinner Tuesday and I go back there once, maybe twice a month for Prostitutes Anonymous [PA] meetings and any other functions that they have. I was also keynote speaker at the graduation this summer." I inquired about the role these relationships played in her life, and her response underscored their therapeutic nature:

> Oh, yes. They're important because they keep you strong. I don't know about anybody else but for me staying connected to where my foundation began is important. It's important that I go back and let other women know that when they leave there they can have a better life, too. I support them not only for me but also to give back.

Although she was unable to visit the PSO as often as she used to, Hayley concurred: "For the longest time I would visit New Horizons about once a week after I graduated, to visit the girls and staff."

Cynthia, one of the few Seeds graduates who still maintained contact with the program, had been out for nine months. She relapsed one month after leaving the program and briefly returned to drugs and prostitution before enrolling in a sober living facility, where she now resided. While she did not get as much support as she desired, she emphasized how important it was to her to maintain this connection. In contrast to the clients of residential PSOs, however, it was extremely challenging for her to maintain a close tie to the program and its staff. Cynthia did not have regular access to members or a site where she could visit, so she resorted to letters or infrequent phone calls with staff. She explained, "Either we talk or I write them or they write me. Once every two weeks they send me a card saying hello. I love that. They send me encouraging words. Even through my relapse I wrote them and told them what was going on and they wrote me back offering support."

Therapeutic Support Groups and Networks

Therapeutic support groups outside of the PSOs, such as 12-step programs, also bolstered clients' lifestyle alterations. These groups were pivotal to women because they comprised a network of supportive individuals invested in recovery, largely centered on the avoidance of past illicit behaviors. Rochelle valued these groups and relationships, as she relied on them to cope with negative feelings and to eschew drug use and prostitution. She stated, "I do go to a lot of meetings. NA, AA, any 'A' that you could name I am there. So there are ways to cope and you don't have to hide behind your feelings there. There are healthy ways to express them and ways to deal with them and what's going on in my life."

Amanda lived in a sober-living apartment complex after leaving New Horizons and regularly attended 12-step programs offered in her building. She found the group's spiritual practices extremely valuable to uphold her new self and corresponding social role: "I go to NA/AA, we have them here in the building. They are really important. What's more important is a spiritual connection with a god of your understanding, as the group encourages . . . because if you don't have that, ain't no AA/NA/PA matter nothing. It's not going to work. You are going to relapse. Go back to the streets."

Cynthia, one of the few Seeds clients who demonstrated any sign of role change, also underscored 12-step meetings as central to her ability to transition into a new life. She believed that her higher power would help her in this process:

> I believe in meetings, fellowships, do my steps. I'm a heavy participant. I still do that today. I feel much freer than I've ever felt. I also know that I have a lot of work to go but that's okay. I'm choosing to look at how far I've come not how far I have to go. I'm very vigilant about my recovery. I do attend fellowship meetings. I go to tons of meetings. I am currently in an outpatient program. I'm very responsible today. I am a mother today to my children. I am a friend today. Someday, not today, I will have a lot to offer in a relationship. I'm going to let God sort them out. Not me.

Upon graduation, Hayley initially attended 12-step meetings regularly for support in her new role. After a couple of years, she still valued and depended on therapeutic relationships but ceased her involvement with 12-step groups. Instead, she turned to PSO graduates and members of her church to maintain her lifestyle transformation. She summarized how these affiliations continued to strengthen her resolve to preserve role and identity changes:

> They helped me learn how to keep myself clean and sober by having different networks and support groups. I also use one of the girls I graduated with from the program when I have problems, or I talk to one of the girls from church. I always use someone to talk about my feelings. I also go to church on the weekends. That helps me out a lot. I don't attend any AA meetings anymore. I stopped a few years ago. Not all meetings are for everyone. I used to go to AA meetings but after a while all you hear is people dwelling on what they were doing. I started losing interest in that. And then I started focusing more on going to church and being in small groups from church, and that's where I found my strength to focus on my future.

Mentoring Others

Recall that in chapter 5, I argued that acting as a mentor (or role model) to other PSO members helped women craft and sustain these changes and socialize others to follow suit. Even after graduating, the act of service continued to provide benefits to those who performed it and cemented their immersion within the newfound role and altered sense of self. Criminologist Shadd Maruna reveals that male offenders who have desisted often make amends by giving back to society. This, he argues, is an important part of the reintegration process.[9] In a similar fashion, the women who desisted in this study dispensed guidance, listened, and offered advice to current program clients, which simultaneously held them accountable for their own behavior even when they no longer lived in the facility. Essentially, it compelled them to practice what they preached.

As I discussed in chapter 4, Felicia regularly mentored PSO residents, a practice that benefited her as well as others. On top of being an informal role model and mentor to novice program members, she also became a 12-step sponsor to a few of the women and volunteered at a local county jail to work with incarcerated women. She felt that all these activities not only kept her on the straight and narrow, but also solidified her new lifestyle removed from drugs and crime:

> One way I've seen myself change is that I became much more humble, much more willing to help new people coming in the program as a result of being in New Horizons. You see, I didn't have very good relationship with women because of something that happened when I was 13 years old so I had a mistrust of women. New Horizons gave me back trust of women. So now I sponsor women that I met at New Horizons . . . actually four of them asked me to be their sponsors once they saw that I had graduated from the program and kept coming back to the Prostitutes Anonymous meetings. I'm also doing volunteer work for a program for incarcerated women.

Amanda likewise volunteered as a mentor because she felt a duty to establish relationships with others in the program: "I'm a mentor to one of the girls at New Horizons. And I think it's important to keep up with the girls who graduate, so they feel connected. So we know how they are doing." Melissa found the support she received from other Phoenix graduates invaluable when she was in the program, so she wanted to continue the practice. She declared, "Basically, I am hoping I can provide inspiration and support that I received when I came in for the new residents that we have here."

Participating in mentorship relationships helps strengthen these lifestyle metamorphoses due to the affective bonds that develop as a result. Other studies highlight the utility of affective bonds as they hold individuals accountable for their actions and deepen their attachment to a role.[10] The bonds exist between PSO clients and staff members, and

also between newer clients and advanced program members or graduates. Melissa's statement underscores her close relationships with other
PSO graduates as they ground her mentally and emotionally. Indeed, she
views these relationships, and the affective ties that ensue, as newfound
coping mechanisms post sex work:

> The previous residents of this program have been the biggest source of
> support for me. Rochelle was here when I first came and then she gradu-
> ated and has her own apartment and, if anybody, she has been my main
> support base. Her and other graduates gave me the inspiration to want to
> do certain things for myself. When I first came in, they were where I am
> at today. And knowing it could be done by seeing them do it is important.
> You know I used to always cope by using [drugs]. I was always smoking
> a pipe or putting a needle in my arm. But now I call friends, by finding
> something that takes my mind off of it. I just try living life on its terms
> now since I'm in a different place.

Rochelle relied on affective relationships with other PSO graduates and
even family members. They helped her cope with difficult emotions and
challenging life circumstances:

> I call friends. I like my phone, I like to get on the phone and call people.
> Just to see what you are doing and if I need to talk about something. My
> children are the most precious things in the world to me. I have to look
> up at my son. But they are mine and they are in my life today. And seeing
> them, the way they see me today is like hell no. I'll never go back. I'll never
> lose that trust in them again.

Amanda concurred that she and other New Horizon graduates make a
point to "keep up with one another for support." And Hayley engages in
similar social practices: "I stay in regular contact with some of the other
graduates who went through the program with me. It's important to my
well-being and theirs to maintain these relationships."

Increasing Human and Social Capital

Beyond establishing and maintaining therapeutic ties to others, another way for women to further solidify their transformations is to build up their human and social capital. They did this by acquiring additional education, a legal career, stable housing, and by cultivating personal interests and future goals aligned with their conventional lifestyle. Based on the findings of countless studies of this population, including this one, it is clear that street prostitutes possess few conventional markers of success. Yet when they received PSO support, many clients increased their human and social capital and continued to prioritize this growth post-graduation.

Educational Attainment and Careers

An overwhelming majority of prostitutes in this sample had minimal educational attainment prior to enrolling in PSOs: 80 percent had not earned a high school diploma, 12.5 percent had, and one woman had an associate's degree in nursing prior to entering prostitution.[11] A lack of educational attainment puts them at a serious disadvantage as they attempt to transition out of sex work and into legal professions. Recognizing this fact, the PSOs strongly encouraged clients to return to school and earn their degrees, as it elevates their chances of employment and increases their self-esteem and self-efficacy. As part of the program expectations, almost all the women who remained in long-term residential programs went back to school to earn credits toward their GED, a specialized certification for a particular occupation, or, in more advanced cases, a college or technical degree.

One study on female desisters reveals that most were unemployed, but instead crafted new identities tied to religion or motherhood (e.g., "Child of God," good mother).[12] In contrast, I find securing stable employment is integral for prostitutes to be able to maintain a life, role, and identity removed from sex work. All of the PSO graduates prioritized employment and educational attainment as key components of their new lifestyles. To that end, those who had high commitment to their new role and identity often continued to advance their educational attainment in order to secure jobs and increase their salaries, all of which deepened their ties to conventional society.

Rochelle explained how the PSO encouraged her education, which helped build her confidence:

> [At first] I didn't know how to work a legit job. I had no skills. They [the PSO] put me through school. I took up computers. I got a certificate and it's like, oh my god, I didn't think I had that in me. I thought that I had lost it. I didn't think I was able to comprehend. And then once I went back to school I began to see that I could comprehend and really understand stuff . . . after that it all changed.

She candidly discussed her fears about being able to succeed at a career outside of prostitution, which she overcame as she slowly acquired the necessary skills to land her current job as a legal assistant:

> Before, I never ever had to be responsible. So the thing that really scared me was getting a real job. You go through stages in the program. First, you get a part-time. That was simple. You don't have to worry because you don't have a bill yet and all your money is going into your little nest egg for when you move. You can bag groceries or something. But then you got to think about a career. Oh, my god, what am I going to do? So I got afraid. I was really scared. What am I going to do, what can I do? And I started doubting myself. I didn't let it get me down though. So I said okay, this is what I'm going to do. I want to work in an office. So I got into a computer class. I went and studied business and English, and I did office procedures. So that helped. After I did that, I landed a job as a legal assistant. And that is what I am today.

Felicia, four years after graduation, was still enrolled in classes to earn her high school diploma and a college degree simultaneously. Throughout this time she also held three part-time jobs, as a loan officer, a nanny, and

a real estate assistant. She subscribed to the belief that advanced education would help her succeed in her career and improve her life overall:

> I'm still working on my GED. I struggled with the GED over the math
> portion and I finally passed that portion. So now I have to take the test on
> science and that's it. Then I'm done with the GED. I managed to pass the
> state law exam in order to become a loan officer. That's a tough task. I'm
> also currently taking justice classes at a community college.

Amanda also emphasized how important additional education and training was for her current job as a cook in the cafeteria of a major hospital,
a position she had held for the past nine months. She stated:

> I appreciate and am truly grateful that I graduated the program. I got
> schooling and a certificate for being a cook with the help of New Horizons.
> Those are things that I never envisioned for myself . . . I accomplished so
> many things in 18 months being at the program that I never did in 47 years
> of my life. They encouraged me to do that and helped me along the way.

Finally, recall Melissa's story at the beginning of this chapter. She believed
that her educational attainment and legal employment were both key factors that enabled her to be able to continue to maintain a conventional
role and identity.

Housing

Securing a place of residence after graduation was crucial for women
to sustain their altered lifestyles. Housing was key for women in their
new lives, given that many had been homeless for much of the time
they worked in prostitution, a condition that further mired them within
street subcultures. Additionally, a safe place to stay enabled them to carry
out tasks that provided stability in their lives, such as work, school, and
12-step meetings.

Of all the PSOs, Phoenix was the only program that owned a nearby apartment complex designated as transitional housing available to program graduates. The rent at these apartments was subsidized by the program and the complex was largely populated by Phoenix graduates. Rochelle had lived in one of the apartments since her graduation, and Melissa was in the process of moving there. The option to move into this housing provided Phoenix clients with a safety net for an extended period after graduation.

Program graduates Amanda, Felicia, and Hayley lived in their own apartments, and Cynthia resided in a room within a state-sponsored sober facility. Unlike the other graduates, who received substantial program aid to acquire housing and employment during their transition, those at Safe Place and Seeds were often left to their own devices. As a result, the women from these two programs struggled to obtain affordable and safe places to reside that served as the foundational block inherent to a transformed lifestyle.

For instance, Cynthia, in particular, felt she needed more treatment after the two-week program offered by Seeds, so she was relieved to get a room in a sober-living house. She found out about the place after finishing the program and relapsing—returning to drugs and street prostitution. After being on a waiting list for some time she finally gained admission, and determined it necessary to her desistance:

> It's good that I'm in a sober-living house with other women. After Seeds, I wanted to live in a sober house with women because I still needed some structure. This place helps me prepare for life in many ways . . . So after the Seeds, what do you have? And if you don't have a support system and it's not just about meetings but it's about women reaching out to women. As women we get intimidated by other women and you need some other women to lift you up. We need a group after Seeds to continue it. It's what happens after—when they leave us—that is key. I go to therapy to deal with issues of sexual molestation. I need more than AA/NA. Seeds may plant the seed but it wasn't enough because I relapsed after I left. That's how I wound up here.

Developing Future Goals and Personal Interests

Mapping out one's future, devising plans, and cultivating personal interests undergirded conventional lifestyles as well. Due to the risks associated with prostitution and addiction, most women claimed they did not think about the future but lived day to day while they were in it. Upon an identity and role transformation, many were able to articulate their goals and the steps they intended to take to achieve them. They were also able to develop and engage in hobbies and pastime activities, a nonexistent luxury when they worked on the streets. The establishment of goals and interests can further cement their commitment to this radically different way of living.

Hayley, for instance, provided the following summary: "I already achieved a lot of my goals—got an apartment, a job, not to drink or use [drugs]. Yeah, I still have two more goals: pass the GED and learn how to drive. My next step is to take the GED over again because I didn't pass last time." Amanda had accomplished a lot of things since leaving the program, but was quick to outline her future objectives: "I've done well but I've got more to go. I want to go back to school again. And I'm saving. I love the fact that my money gets taken out and I pay my rent, phone, and cable all by myself."

Rochelle listed her short- and long-term goals but emphasized that she needed to view each as part of a longer process so she would not get discouraged and return to the streets.

My future goals are to continue to stay clean and sober to better my education. I'm going to try to become a paralegal. I'm looking into schools to see which school will be better and how long it takes. So I have to work on all that. That's my short-time goal: Work on school, get into school. I don't try to overload myself because that will set you up for failure. So I take one step at a time. That's something Phoenix has taught me. You don't put too much on your plate. If you don't do what's on your plate it upsets you, and then you feel that you are less than, you're nothing, you can't do stuff. So I take baby steps. Once I take that step, I take another step. That's where

I find myself to grow when I take baby steps and then that step and then that step. That's how I stay true to the real me and who I am.

On top of these goals, she described the hobbies she discovered, which are indicative of her current identity. Her attainment of goals, harboring future ones, and hobbies and leisure activities all fortified these changes.

In the program, I realized I love books. And every Christmas I get a book from Sally [the program director]. And that helped me cope. I do journal. I write. I started writing when I was living there. I look back on my journals and I think, did I really used to think that? But I still journal today. So that's a way of coping. I still read. I love reading. I think I'm a workaholic today. I love my job. I clean up. I take walks. I still do meetings. All of these things are new for me, and I didn't do them while I was out there [in prostitution]. They are part of my new life and the new me.

Melissa not only juxtaposed her former life to her current one, but was able to articulate numerous future goals as well. The evolution of her thinking is also apparent in the following account:

When I first came to the program my mind was mostly just try to get through the program. I wasn't thinking about my future. I was thinking about what I need to do immediately right now. Now I look ahead in my life. Back then I was just going from day to day trying to stay clean because it was hard. My future goal now is number one to stay clean and sober and off the streets. My second goal would be to maintain the same job I'm at or a better job. Keep my apartment. Buy me a car. To be able to start visiting my sons or having them come out and visit me. They both want to come out and visit me when I move into my apartment.

Establishing aspirations and plans encourages women to retain focus on the future and enriches their dedication to conventional lifestyles.

Do These Alterations Last? Permanency of Role Exits

I now want to revisit the question I posed earlier in the chapter—the issue of long-term exits from prostitution. There is always the possibility that economic, social, or personal circumstances can pull women back into street prostitution (and their former role and identity). However, the aforementioned activities and foci work as anchors to help shore up conventional lifestyles, roles, and identities for the women. As I detailed in chapter 5, individual commitment to such changes is also central to the desistance process, which can be elevated by the number of "side bets" or perceived benefits the individual stands to gain from the new role.[13] For example, a woman can view a legal job as a way to elevate her social and economic status, generate human and social capital, and enhance her self-worth and self-esteem. Conversely, if she does not recognize the benefits associated with this conventional occupation, or simply places no value on them, she is less devoted to it and runs the risk of returning to her prior role of prostitution.

Despite the possibility of reverting to a former role, scholars assert that individuals who adopt organizationally fostered roles and identities are typically invested in maintaining them. As organizational scholars John Van Maanen and Edgar Schein explain: "Once a person has successfully completed a difficult divestiture process and has constructed something of a new identity based on the role to which the divestiture process was directed, there are strong forces toward the maintenance of the new identity."[14] Sociologist Teela Sanders concludes that sex workers generally do not become involved in other acts of deviancy once they have exited the trade, and they tend to keep their past history a secret in order to eschew stigmatization, negative labels, and discrimination.[15] For those who experience role exits while in PSOs, the forces that undergird such alterations consist of their ongoing connections to programs and others who validate their new role and identity, a determination to increase their capital, and sustained high levels of commitment to this new lifestyle.

Without longitudinal data following the women in this sample, I cannot make unequivocal claims of long-term desistance or their avoidance of future acts of deviance and crime indefinitely. However, the cases of certain PSO graduates—including Felicia, Hayley, Melissa, Amanda, Cynthia, and Rochelle—suggest that exits from street prostitution and the maintenance of conventional lifestyles (roles and identities) are possible and even longstanding. Continued empirical investigation of the permanency of these exits is needed to further address these concerns.

Recommendations: Legislation, Behavior, and Organizations

Recall the three main theoretical perspectives on prostitution, where each one articulates an ideological view: The first is the oppression paradigm, a stance that considers all types of sex work exploitative due to patriarchal conditions, and harmful to those who participate in it.[16] The second is the empowerment paradigm, which frames prostitution as a form of labor and one that can potentially enhance the lives of those who choose to perform it.[17] The final perspective, the polymorphous paradigm, asserts that sex work is complex and varied, resulting in no uniform experience. It takes into account the specific working conditions and other sociostructural arrangements that shape the experiences of this population.[18] Yet even across these diverse paradigms there is acknowledgment that street prostitution is the most volatile, dangerous, and risky form of sex work. As a group, these individuals experience disproportionately high rates of violence, arrest, incarceration, stigmatization, and drug use vis-à-vis other sex workers.

Despite the negative outcomes associated with the trade, street prostitution continues to be a prevalent feature of contemporary American society; punitive laws persist, and financial costs for arrests, legal and judicial processing, and incarceration soar. Thus many Americans argue that prostitution is a social problem in dire need of a solution. What, if anything, can be done to improve the lives of those who engage in prostitution? Are there ways to remedy—or at least lessen—the legal, criminological, and social implications that arise from outdoor sex work?

Changing Legislation

The legality of prostitution varies considerably across the world. Consequently, these sociolegal configurations engender strikingly different experiences for prostitutes. One such model embraces legalization or decriminalization.[19] Numerous countries have implemented this approach and have passed laws intended to enhance the safety of workers and lessen discriminatory practices against them, including New Zealand, Canada, Australia, some Mexican states, and much of Europe, including the Netherlands.[20] In most of these settings, however, the laws apply only to indoor sex workers, a deliberate plan to urge street-level prostitutes to move out of the public eye.

An alternative model is far more punitive. Prevalent in the United States, this strategy focuses on containment and punishment directed toward those who engage in prostitution, a policy that often confers a myriad of negative consequences onto them.[21] Of course, the most visible sex workers, street prostitutes, tend to be the most impacted by such practices, and commonly experience multiple arrests, jail sentences, extensive criminal records, and stigmatizing labels, all of which can preclude, or at least impede, their transition out of the trade. To make matters more challenging, the fear of being apprehended and criminalized relegates outdoor prostitutes and sex acts to dark corners, practices that heighten their risk of physical and sexual violence.

Much of the public castigates prostitution due to pervasive moral beliefs about the work. Undergirding this sentiment is the longstanding cultural precept that women should not use their sexuality for profit. There are also a host of other crimes that coincide with outdoor sex work, including disorderly conduct, greater trash and noise, increased harassment of women, and loss of merchant business, all of which fuel omnipresent negative social opinions about this population.[22] Moral outrage, coupled with the rise in related crimes in neighborhoods where prostitutes work, intensify citizen pressure on legislators and law enforcement to crack down on them, which is done almost exclusively through arrests, removal, and punitive practices.

When it comes to intellectuals, scholars offer diverse and often contradictory recommendations concerning legislation of prostitution. Some strongly oppose decriminalization and legalization based on the argument that such legislation will condone, and even exacerbate, the mistreatment and exploitation of female prostitutes. Most of these individuals highlight the victimization of prostitutes, espouse a desire to eradicate the structural and personal reasons for entrance into the trade, and prompt their exits. However, the practical recommendations of how precisely to end it often remain unformulated or exceptionally difficult to implement.

In contrast, others propose that structural changes in the guise of legalization or decriminalization will offer institutional protections for prostitutes, thereby lessening their mistreatment while granting them additional labor rights. Proponents of this concept believe that prostitution is a viable work option for individuals, which the current laws deny. Although a daunting task, liberalizing legislation may hold the potential to offset some of the hardships street prostitutes routinely face, and reduce a portion of the financial burden that results from policing, prosecuting, and incarcerating them. Certain researchers argue that decriminalization and legalization policies ameliorate at least a modicum of the disadvantages and discriminatory practices experienced by prostitutes. A few empirical studies uphold this assertion.

Sociologists Barbara Brents, Crystal Jackson, and Kathryn Hausbeck studied legal brothels in Nevada and conclude that these women report much safer working conditions and well-being compared to street workers.[23] Of course, the obvious difference between the two populations is that the former perform sex acts indoors while the latter operate in public arenas. Yet the central linchpin in these differential experiences is the extent of regulation that is imposed onto them.

In an international study, sociologist Ronald Weitzer finds that most sex workers situated in the red light district in Amsterdam report feeling safer in these legalized, highly controlled contexts.[24] Indeed, there is a police presence in this setting that keeps an eye on untoward clients and settles disturbances. Proponents of more liberal prostitution laws believe that regulated working conditions can grant sex workers increased legal and physical protections, which is also beneficial for the larger community. Supporters draw on these empirical cases, among others, to promote their assertion that widespread legalization or decriminalization offers advantages for everyone: The prostitutes are safer, there is less violence and drug use among them, they are healthier, the public is sheltered from public sex acts and the associated crimes that ensue because the work largely moves indoors, and such measures can also alleviate some of the costs and energy the criminal justice system currently expends to prosecute and penalize them.

Certain American cities and international countries (e.g., Sweden) also apply legal and punitive measures on customers, with the intention of deterring their future solicitation of prostitutes. Sociologists Barbara Brents and colleagues argue that the United States relies on a combination of prohibitionist (selling sex is illegal and the prostitute is punished) *and* abolitionist (punishments are directed at third parties, not sex workers) policies.[25] These strategies therefore attack both the supply and demand side of outdoor sex work.

To better understand the latter, sociologist Martin Monto conducted research on the customers of prostitutes.[26] His work explores the variety of punishments directed at clients to dissuade any future consumption of sex work, including arrests and fines, car impounds, and public shaming tactics (e.g., mug shots and charges printed in a local newspaper).[27] Some US cities also sponsor "john schools" established by the court system, criminal justice agencies, and other organizations, which clients attend as part of their court sentence. These schools are designed to educate solicitors about the harms of prostitution and hold them accountable for their contribution to the phenomenon of sex work.[28] Completing the class and paying a fine enables individuals to avoid arrest records and court trials, yet attending them constitutes a form of public shaming. Moreover, as family science scholar Rochelle Dalla points out, it is unclear whether john schools actually generate long-lasting behavioral changes among consumers.[29] Nevertheless, the practice of doling out punishment to customers is a recent trend in the United States and other countries, such as Sweden, that appears to be gaining public endorsement.[30]

Despite the growing demand for client accountability, much of the American public continues to attribute blame to the sex workers and endorses prohibitionist policies and practices. This strong social disapproval shores up the sustained criminalization of this population, which in turn generates ongoing cycles of arrests, incarceration, and release and return to sex work, with few alternative options available. Because of the entrenched cultural, political, and social climates in the United States regarding prostitution, legislative changes are extremely unlikely to transpire in the near future. Recognizing this quagmire, Ronald Weitzer outlines a two-track policy for the United States that was originally devised in Britain in the mid-twentieth century. This includes the following changes: (1) targeting resources toward the reduction of street prostitution, and (2) lessening enforcement against indoor actors who operate consensually.[31] In other words, he asserts that in a society where the liberalization of laws are doubtful, this two-track policy could offer enhanced protections for women and increase exits among street workers, who face the greatest number of risks, while allowing indoor prostitution to occur de facto.

Incorporating Protective Measures in Communities

Chapter 2 included statements from women who indicated that in the neighborhoods where they grew up prostitution was omnipresent and a socially acceptable activity, a perception that contributed to their entrance into the trade. In certain cases, the benefits of street prostitution were significant upon entry but over time the negative consequences—drug addiction, violence and assault, criminalization, stigmatization, and homelessness—grew and ultimately offset these gains. Many of the undesirable outcomes emerged from the ecological conditions in which they worked—high-risk areas of the city rife with criminal activities and violence.

In the previous section, I discussed how legalization and decriminalization could serve to potentially enhance the safety and well-being of sex workers. Since this is improbable in the United States, another tactic would be to improve the conditions of the work environments or modify the behaviors of the workers immersed within such settings. There are many law enforcement attempts to clean up areas of cities where prostitution thrives, but in effect this often just displaces and relocates prostitutes to other areas that offer similar criminal elements, where they hope to avoid detection and criminalization.[32]

If we assume that these ecological conditions will remain in pockets of most American cities, then an alternative—and more practical—approach would be to focus on encouraging different behaviors among prostitutes to elevate their safety. One way to do so is via prostitute-serving organizations (PSOs), which are typically situated in or near major urban areas in order to best serve this population. These programs can influence the behaviors of street prostitutes by disseminating information about precautionary measures, distributing resources that uphold this aim, and offering intervention services to those who want to leave the lifestyle altogether. Although the directives and services of PSOs vary considerably, those that attempt to mitigate the harms prostitutes face carry out one or more of the following tasks: communicating what constitutes safe sex act practices (e.g., the buddy system); distributing free condoms and offering STD tests or advice on treatment options; and providing temporary shelter, minor medical care, and referrals to social workers or health care clinics. We do not yet know the extent to which these programs assuage ecological risks for this population, yet they may be the only (or primary) agent that fulfills this function for them, as many of the women in this study report. If that is indeed the case, the outreach and services of PSOs may be an important contributor to the well-being and safety of street prostitutes overall.

While some studies unearth that police can be perpetrators of harm and violence against street prostitutes, they also hold the potential to act as catalysts to improve prostitutes' lives and working conditions. Officers who have regular contact with prostitutes could direct them to service agencies, PSOs, or clinics when they need aid or desire to alter their lifestyles— in other words, they can act as bridges. As I noted in chapter 3, in some instances police officers even physically transport women to PSOs rather than arrest them, in an effort to remove them from the streets. Greater collaboration between PSOs and officers can make this type of connection a routine practice. Police officers can also keep prostitutes informed about violent crimes that occur in their area and pass along descriptions of alleged perpetrators, so the women can be more vigilant in screening customers.

Currently prostitutes often avoid the police when they need protection for fear of criminalization. But police, as discretionary enforcers of the law, have the power to erect a different relationship with this vulnerable population—to become someone who offers resources, aid, and protection. A way to foster this type of interaction is to require officers to undergo educational training where they acquire a thorough understanding of the hardships street prostitutes face, are encouraged to build rapport with them, and learn about the local resources able to address their needs. If such changes transpired, prostitutes' perceptions of law enforcement might shift to the point where they view the police as allies more than foes. This is especially important when it comes to those who are trafficked or forced to perform sex work against their will, increasing the chances they will turn to police for help if the opportunity arises.

PSOs and Social Movements as Agents of Change

Many scholars attribute the phenomenon of street-level sex work to structural and economic constraints such as extreme poverty, low educational attainment, lack of social capital, and few career choices.[33] Once these limitations are overcome, prostitutes will experience expanded options regarding careers that may influence their tenure in the trade. That accomplishment, however, is no easy feat. Due to the background characteristics that many street prostitutes share, it is exceptionally difficult for them to acquire conventional skill sets in order to experience upward mobility without help from outsiders.

In her book *Exposing the "Pretty Woman" Myth: A Qualitative Investigation of Street-Level Prostituted Women*, scholar Rochelle Dalla stresses the role that organizations play in promoting these transitions. In order to improve the effectiveness of such programs, she points out the necessity of academic studies that analyze the overall exiting process for this population: "This type of information is critical if intervention services are to effectively address challenges associated with the exit process as women attempt to forge new lives for themselves away from the 'game.'"[34] As I have demonstrated throughout this book, PSOs can directly impact prostitutes and their quality of life by shepherding them through the process of attaining the necessary skills and credentials that lead to conventional lifestyles. PSOs are unique because they are the only organizations that provide support and resources specifically tailored to the needs of this population, often with the intention to build human and social capital.

The ability to deliver such services is a substantial challenge for these nonprofit programs, as they are typically underfunded, which limits the number of individuals they can help. Despite the consensus that prostitution is indeed a widespread social problem, the federal, state, and local governments provide minimal funding to directly aid prostitutes or facilitate their exits from the trade. Thus the viability of PSOs, the extent of their services, and the number of individuals they assist depends largely on their fundraising abilities, spanning both the private and public sectors. Their success in this endeavor fluctuates dramatically and is closely tied to the strength of the economy. However, if the US government viewed PSOs as a possible solution to tackle this problem—assuming the programs demonstrate success in generating exits—then they could set aside funding to these programs to ensure their survival, and even expand the number of them nationwide to meet the high demand. Such allocation could accomplish multiple goals: to get more individuals out of street prostitution, and alleviate the costs of policing, prosecuting, and incarcerating these individuals.

Amending legislation, improving safety skills of street sex workers, increasing resources to PSOs, and expanding the number of programs nationwide all harbor the potential to address the prevalent practice of street prostitution and the undesirable outcomes associated with it. These changes may be even more critical when it comes to helping trafficked people— those forced to engage in sex work against their will. There could feasibly be future PSOs that target especially vulnerable populations, such as youth or trafficked individuals.[35] Unfortunately, none of these alterations are likely to occur without substantial external support. Social movement and advocacy organizations may act as catalysts to draw increased public attention to these issues, and exert greater pressure on legislators, the government, and the criminal justice system to institute changes that move beyond the status quo. We have recently witnessed some development in this regard pertaining to those who are trafficked, but there is still a general lack of attention on nontrafficked domestic street prostitutes in the United States.

Overall, we have minimal empirically driven knowledge of the ways that social movement and advocacy organizations have elicited social, political, and cultural changes regarding prostitution.[36] A few scholars have started to examine this topic, but most employ an international focus. Based on her historical comparative study of international organizations that shape prostitution policies, sociologist Stephanie Limoncelli concludes that they often espouse the dominant paradigm regarding sex work, which is typically prohibitionist or absolutist in nature.[37] However, she calls for further analyses of such organizations' competing political and ideological positions and activities to further flush this out. In another international study, anthropologist Jeanett Bjønness explores how various Danish institutional actors (including nongovernmental organizations or NGOs) have impacted the public discourse on prostitution. Her work reveals that they espouse either the oppression or empowerment viewpoints on sex work, but the former perspective is the prevailing and dominant public stance.[38]

When it comes to US organizations and their ability to cultivate social, political, and cultural alterations regarding prostitution, there are only a handful of studies that address this issue, and most focus exclusively on social movement organizations (e.g., the prostitutes' rights movement).[39] In a recent article, sociologist Ronald Weitzer and I analyze the extent to which PSOs engage in advocacy work. While all PSOs provide services to prostitutes—a basic organizational objective—some also perform advocacy to amend public perceptions and legislation that impact this group. These organizations differ from social movements, given that their primary purpose is to allocate aid and resources to enhance the quality of life for prostitutes, and advocacy, when it is done, is secondary. We unearth the factors that account for a PSO's ability to do both, which include (1) whether they establish a clear target and remedy, and (2) whether they have developed ties to ideologically aligned advocacy organizations (such as social movements).[40] In a similar vein, political scientist Samantha Majic conducted case studies on two domestic PSOs to examine whether they bring about social change that affects prostitutes.[41] Scholars who conduct research on this population recommend increased advocacy efforts at state, national, and international levels in order to elevate their safety and lessen their discrimination and mistreatment by the public and the criminal justice system.

Conclusion

There are few resources for prostitutes to draw on to cultivate their transition out of the trade. While the women in this study did at times use other public and nonprofit agencies out of necessity, such as health clinics or homeless shelters, PSOs uniquely offered services tailored to their needs. Furthermore, most women were reluctant to utilize other aid organizations because they found them largely inadequate: They were overpopulated, flawed, did not provide the services they desired; they had incompetent, racist, or uncaring staff members; they were rife with criminal activities, such as drug use; or they were unsafe settings for women. PSOs are but one method for females to leave sex work, and, as my study indicates, the programs varied considerably in terms of their effectiveness in generating such transformations.

Besides PSOs, Rochelle Dalla identifies alternative pathways prostitutes use to exit: Some leave on their own, with help from family members, or desist while incarcerated.[42] We do not know the success of these trajectories vis-à-vis exits through PSOs. However, the prostitutes in this sample vociferously stated they would not have been able to leave without help from PSOs given their circumstances and backgrounds (e.g., little educational attainment, criminal records, stigma, addiction, trauma, lack of social networks and resources). Those who had attempted to stop in the past on their own or while in prison were unable to sustain these changes for any length of time and quickly returned to the streets. Moreover, most women did not have family members who were willing or capable of providing the substantial resources and skills it took for them to transition into conventional lifestyles. In short, my analysis suggests that particular PSOs, with specific cultures and structures, constitute ideal sites to facilitate exits for street prostitutes compared to other pathways. Additional social science research is necessary to further examine this topic and substantiate this claim.

Phoenix, Safe Place, and Seeds still operate today and carry out much of the same work. New Horizons, however, had a different fate and was shut down in 2006 due to embezzlement committed by a few members of the upper management. This was a shocking revelation to the rest of the staff and clients. Many of the women in the residential program were turned out into the streets with little warning and with nowhere to go. There were no comparable programs in the city of Chicago that served their multifaceted needs of housing, food, therapy, counseling, staff oversight and guidance, drug addiction treatment, educational attainment, and protection from the temptations of street life. In response to this closure, another religious social service agency in the city created an outreach and service program in 2007 and 2008 for prostitutes that primarily targeted addiction and STDs. It is unclear if this program still exists today, and in what capacity. In an effort to acquire more information, I repeatedly tried to call the program this past year but was unable to make contact, and there is no current information available online. Based on what I was able to learn about this program from outdated online information, it offered significantly fewer services to street prostitutes and had no residential facilities.

I hope this book provides readers better insight into the experiences of street prostitutes across multiple US cities, many of whom espoused a desire to quit and a litany of reasons to do so. Given their abundant social, economic, and occupational disadvantages, this is a formidable transition to undertake. As my research demonstrates, exiting is a complex process that unfolds over time and one that is significantly shaped by organizational cultures, structures, and practices. Yet it is important to recognize that the women all display some degree of agency as they resist or embrace a new lifestyle.

PSOs are neither the only solution nor are they guaranteed—some women still fall out of the program or refuse to implement changes. It is clear, however, that PSOs can act as agents of change to improve the quality of life for those who remain in the trade and to expedite exits among those who desire them. As a society we need to recognize and consider all the options, and I find that PSOs hold great potential to meet prostitutes where they practice, address their circumstances, and usher them into conventional lifestyles. When successful, these programs help individuals overcome structural, social, and personal barriers, which is a laudable and extremely valuable enterprise.

METHODOLOGICAL APPENDIX

As I discussed earlier in the book, I was able to access PSOs due to my gender, credentials, and social networks. I was able to "flaunt it when I got it"—a phrase borrowed from Julie Mazzei and Erin O'Brien that refers to a field researcher's ability to use her or his gender in order to build rapport and gain analytic advantage while in the field.[1] Due to the belief that female prostitutes have problematic relationships with men in general, many PSOs are staffed and run by women. Additionally, it is a common practice of residential programs to limit interactions between female clients and males for periods of time, assuming that such exchanges will reify entrenched unhealthy behavioral patterns. Because of my gender I was able to gain access to these sites and freely interact with female prostitutes, often with little oversight from staff members. It also enabled me to form connections with clients based upon our shared gender and commonalities, despite our divergent histories. For instance, many women wanted to discuss fashion, beauty, appearance, ways to combat weight gain, relationships with significant others, and so forth. As for the gatekeepers (e.g., PSO staff members), my academic affiliation, knowledge, and past interactions with PSOs granted me credibility. Based upon the assumption that I was an "expert," staff members frequently sought my opinion and input about clients and their program.

Although I was open about my role as an academic researcher, and while it seemed to garner staff respect, this fact was surprisingly insignificant among clients. Most women were gregarious, open, and friendly when interacting with me, even after they learned that I was studying them and their PSO. Before long, I was privy to personal feelings, stories, family and background histories, and even criticisms of the program and staff. Despite these inroads, I still occupied a liminal outsider position situated between a client and staff member; I was neither in a position of authority nor one subjected to rules and staff supervision. While a delicate balancing act, my regular and sustained presence at each PSO over time, the personal relationships I developed with both staff and clients, and the trust that ensued allowed me to navigate and gain access to both worlds simultaneously. This flexibility was extremely valuable during my fieldwork and to my research overall, as it allowed me to collect rich data at each site from two divergent perspectives. In the rare cases where clients were reluctant to conduct formal interviews with me, even the most recalcitrant individual engaged in informal conversations with me by the end of my fieldwork.

I inhabited multiple roles and carried out numerous tasks while immersed at these settings. At each site, staff members asked me to lead at least one class on a particular topic, when I was qualified and willing to do so. This task placed me in a position of authority, yet given the infrequency with which I completed it, did not appear to change the dynamics between clients and myself. For much of the time, I remained a participant observer and went through the daily activities with the women such as eating meals, cooking, attending classes and group sessions, spending free time talking and joking, having one-on-one conversations, and helping them with homework. Occasionally I ran errands for staff members or clients, completed administrative duties, or attended staff meetings, but such activities consumed a small fraction of my overall time at these sites.

The comparative ethnographic approach I used in this book enabled me to tease out differences among PSOs and analyze the ways in which organizations influenced the process of exiting sex work. Relying on a grounded theory, initially coined by Barney Glaser and Anselm Strauss, my research insights inductively emerged from the ethnographic fieldwork data and interviews I collected at each site location.[2] As Gideon Kunda notes, "The strength of ethnography is its concern with detail: limited settings, routines, everyday life, and strive to understand the 'native point of view.'"[3] In spite of this contribution, ethnography also poses limitations to social science research, as it may be more challenging to generalize across settings and populations. This study focuses on four distinct PSOs and samples of prostitutes, and how the subsequent dynamics engender patterns of talk and behavior that may or may not lead to role exits. While we must be cautious about overgeneralizing to all prostitute-serving organizations or all female street prostitutes, the findings in this book can be used as a starting point to prompt further investigation into similar programs and exiting trajectories.

Finally, the data in this book were collected between 2002 and 2006. The current structures, staff members, and practices of the PSOs since that time may have shifted slightly, and as I pointed out, one of these organizations is now closed. Nevertheless, the four sites constitute representative types of PSOs that exist within the United States.

New Horizons

New Horizons was a nonprofit PSO located in a crime-ridden Chicago neighborhood, situated a mile or so from a notorious prostitution stroll. In the fall of 2005 when I conducted my fieldwork, the program had been in existence for 22 years, although it had moved locations a few times over that period. I conducted ethnography from September through December of that year, attending the program four to five full days per week. New Horizons employed close to 20 staff members, at least half of whom were in full-time paid positions, and there were a handful of unpaid volunteers and interns scattered across various departments. The program also had a board of directors comprised of 24 members, who met regularly to discuss operations, funding, and the program trajectory.

The PSO offered a range of services and programs tailored to meet the needs of female prostitutes, including a residential treatment facility, a crisis shelter, and street and jail outreach. The residential program, which is the main focus of this study, occupied the second and third floor of one of two adjoining buildings. The administrative staff and offices were positioned in the other building, and there was limited interaction between the office staff and residential staff and clients. The residential program housed up to 18 women at one time for the duration of 18 to 24 months. New Horizons provided room and board to clients, as well as extra expenses such as clothing, travel costs, and a meager allowance. Due to space constraints, two women shared each room.

The program emulated a total institution model for novice clients, due to a rigidly controlled environment where staff members continually monitored residents, and there were limitations placed upon clients' physical movement off the premises. Initially residents were prohibited to leave the house unchaperoned, but as they advanced in the program they were able to gain increased freedom in order to work or attend school without supervision. Clients entered the program due to court mandates and intervention from an authority figure (e.g., a judge, lawyer, parole officer, or social worker), or they entered on their own volition.

The organizational objectives included getting women to leave prostitution by progressing through the residential program, and ultimately to acquire conventional markers of success, including educational credentials, a legal occupation, and sobriety. In order to attain these goals, New Horizons, like many nonprofit agencies, was quite preoccupied with securing funding to continue to operate and serve prostitutes. This PSO received revenue from a variety of private and public sources: state, federal, private foundations, and personal donations. One noteworthy source of funding—and a point of pride among both the staff and clients—was a sizeable grant from the Oprah Winfrey Foundation that spanned two years.

New Horizons worked closely with law enforcement and the court system, and made it a point to establish and expand the number of these collaborative relationships. Their recently opened "john school" (a day-long class intended for men who were caught soliciting a prostitute) resulted from multiagency cooperation between New Horizons, the city police department, and criminal court judges. Due to this arrangement, men arrested for soliciting prostitutes were court-ordered to attend a full-day workshop that discussed the potential dangers associated with prostitutes, and to pay a $500 fee to New Horizons. All these parties benefitted from this arrangement—the police and courts believed it would help deter customers from soliciting prostitutes in the future (and ostensibly reduce prostitution activities), and the PSO received revenue to continue to operate. New Horizons also held regular community fundraisers and educational events to create awareness of the program in order to boost donations.

Despite the number of programs offered and the many individuals who utilized their services, New Horizons closed in the spring of 2006 due to a financial scandal involving the program director and other top staff members. All operations ceased at this time, including the residential facility, and the staff was laid off. After a lengthy court trial, the director was charged with embezzlement, had to pay restitution, and was sentenced to prison for one year.

Phoenix

Phoenix is a nonprofit PSO situated in a northern suburban city of Los Angeles, California. Like New Horizons, Phoenix operated a residential facility for female prostitutes, located in a two-story house in a suburban neighborhood that is undistinguishable from the other houses on the block. There was also a small office located at a different facility in a nearby city. The program was founded in 1980, and with 33 years of operation, it remains one of the oldest programs in the nation that directly serves female prostitutes. I conducted ethnographic fieldwork at this site beginning in August of 2002 and finished in January 2003. I visited one or two times per week for the period, and remained for close to eight hours during each visit. At that time there were three full-time residential staff members and three part-timers who worked at the office location, but they had little direct interaction with clients. The board of directors consisted of 11 individuals who oversaw staff members and program operations, with a primary focus of fundraising for the program to continue to operate.

Phoenix operated a long-term residential program for prostitutes that lasted up to two years. They only housed up to six women at one time due to space constraints. The program covered the costs of room and board, travel expenses, and offered allowances to residents in exchange for chores. Once clients secured a part-time job, however, they were required to pay for a portion of their expenses. Phoenix also owned a shared living community in a nearby city—an apartment complex reserved for program graduates, who could reside there and pay a subsidized rent for an unlimited duration of time. Clients were either mandated to the program by a judge, lawyer, parole officer, or social worker, or voluntarily enrolled on their own accord. Unlike New Horizons, Phoenix did not offer other services, such as street outreach or a john school, and the director and few staff members did not have the resources or energy to invest in building relationships with members of the criminal justice system, such as lawyers, lawmakers, police or judges.

Phoenix also embraced a total institutional setting, one that allowed clients more autonomy and freedom as they moved through the program and earned the trust of the staff. Therefore, at the onset they were unable to freely leave the premises without supervision and had to receive approval to attend outside appointments or enroll in educational classes. A primary organizational goal was to facilitate client exits out of prostitution. Their approach was to slowly reintegrate clients into society by helping them acquire education, job training, housing, and legitimate jobs.

Phoenix received no government assistance and instead depended on donations from private foundations, organizations, churches, and patrons, because they wanted to maintain flexibility and be unencumbered by federal and state restrictions. They also held occasional events in the community to disseminate information about the program and help bolster additional resources and funds. Phoenix still operates today, continues to offer both residential and off-site housing programs, and has even expanded their services to include a drop-in clinic and a family reunification program.

Safe Place

The third site, Safe Place, is a 12-year-old nonprofit program located in the affluent suburbs of Minneapolis-St. Paul, Minnesota. It is run by a larger umbrella organization that sponsors numerous social service agencies and programs. Safe Place also operated a residential facility, which was initially established due to collaboration with a Catholic religious organization that owns the building and land and leases it to Safe Place because they serve a disadvantaged population. I conducted fieldwork at this location for two and a half months during the summer of 2006. While I was there for a shorter duration of time, I was highly immersed within this setting and attended the site approximately five days a week, for six to eight hours per visit. The staff consisted of seven full-time employees and a handful of volunteer and part-time employees. Safe Place did not have a board of directors assigned to oversee this program; instead, the program vision and trajectory was primarily left to the program founder, director, and a select group of staff members.

Safe Place offered only a residential program for women involved in prostitution, with a special focus on treating their substance abuse. It occupied two large buildings situated on 60 acres of rural land, surrounded by woods and within walking distance to a small lake. This residential program housed up to a 15 women at one time, and each woman could reside for a maximum of three months. Safe Place provided their meals, bills, and living expenses while they were enrolled in the program.

Although there was 24-hour staff supervision of clients, a practice reminiscent of total institutions, most of the other characteristics of such an organization were absent. Beyond limitations imposed on clients' physical movement, the overall structure, rules, and organizational goals at Safe Place were vague and undeveloped compared to New Horizons and Phoenix. Indeed, there were general inconsistencies and contradictions when it came to the expectations placed upon clients, the rules that governed their behavior, and discipline for rule infractions. The staff encouraged clients to establish their own goals and find ways to accomplish them, which typically resulted in minimal client progress and change.

Safe Place received almost all of their funding from the state of Minnesota, with very few private donations, thus making them highly dependent on state support to maintain their services. They initially were awarded a large start-up grant from the state to establish the residential program, and, as of 2006, received state funding for each woman in the program, which sustained daily operations. The program did have an informal connection to the criminal justice system, because the director of Safe Place also worked at a nearby prison program for female inmates. To that end, she acted as a liaison and recommended particular women with a history of prostitution to attend the program. Yet this recruitment strategy was entirely contingent upon her abilities. Most clients were mandated to attend Safe Place through court order, although some asked to gain acceptance to the program. Safe Place continues to serve this population today.

Seeds

The last site, Seeds, is located in the vicinity near Hartford, Connecticut. This 33-year-old nonprofit PSO offered a variety of services and programs to prostitutes and those at risk for it: street outreach, a two-week program for women convicted of prostitution charges, and educational talks to local schools about the dangers of the sex trade. The core service of Seeds, and the focus of this study, is the two-week class for women convicted of prostitution charges. I conducted ethnography at this site from January through March of 2006 when I attended the program five days per week, approximately eight hours per day. There were four full-time and three part-time staff members who worked at Seeds. The board of directors had five members, a few of whom were also full-time staff.

There was a cooperative relationship between Seeds and the criminal court system, where women facing prostitution charges were sentenced to this program as an alternative to prison or jail sentences. A court-mandated sentence was the only mode of entrée into this program. There were typically between five to ten women enrolled per class, but often these numbers shrank over the course of the two weeks as women fell out of the program. Of course, when they did so, they violated their sentences and received a bench warrant.

Seeds was similar to a therapeutic support group where the staff members served to facilitate conversations and self-reflection among clients. While they attempted to build clients' self-esteem and discussed alternative options to sex work, there were no uniform organizational objectives. Instead, they allowed the clients to establish their own goals, and encouraged them to achieve them. Only two staff members participated in this program and therefore had the most interaction with the clients. They hoped to plant a seed of change within their clients, but were quick to point out the limitations of this short program. The staff members tried to maintain some contact with program graduates, but it was uncommon for many of these relationships to persist. Whereas all the other PSOs had an on-site social worker or counselor, Seeds had no such staff person available.

Seeds almost exclusively received its funding from state and federal sources, with very minimal private donations. They received a few large federal grants during my fieldwork, funds which supplemented the state-allotted payment for each woman who enrolled in their program. Seeds continues to operate today and offers many of the same program services to those engaged in prostitution.

NOTES

NOTES TO CHAPTER 1

1. The terms "client," "customer," "trick," and "john" are all used interchangeably throughout this book, and all refer to male consumers of sex acts. Female sex workers typically cite the latter two terms.

2. Some scholars take umbrage at the use of the term "prostitute" because they feel it connotes a negative, stigmatized social position for these individuals. Instead, they use "sex worker," a more neutral term. I deliberately chose to use "prostitute" throughout this book, although at times I also use "sex worker" to refer to this population. When I use "prostitute" my intention is not to label or further stigmatize these women, but because I feel that "sex worker" encompasses a vastly diverse group of individuals including strippers, escorts, phone sex workers, porn actresses, and street prostitutes. My findings and analyses are specific to female street prostitutes; therefore, I am unable to generalize to other categories of sex workers and do not want to use language that glosses over their differences.

3. While these studies are still sparse, a handful of academics have begun to examine male and transgendered sex workers (see Aggleton 1999, Kaye 2003, and West 1993).

4. Delacoste and Alexander (1998).

5. Rosen and Venkatesh (2008).

6. Porter and Bonilla (2010), Raphael and Shapiro (2002), and Weitzer (1999).

7. Bourgois and Dunlap (1993), Miller (1995), and Pearl (1987).

8. Alexander (1987).

9. Alexander (1987), Arnold et al. (2000), Dalla (2000), Epele (2001), Forbes (1993), and Porter and Bonilla (2010).

10. US Department of Justice (2001).

11. For a comprehensive review of this debate, see Barton (2006) and Chapkis (1997).

12. Bernstein (2007), Dewey (2010), Sanders (2005), and Weitzer (2010).

13. Dalla (2000).

14. Dalla (2006), Månsson and Hedin (1999), and Sanders (2007).

15. Dalla (2006), Davis (2000), Murphy and Venkatesh (2006), and Weitzer (2000).

16. Baker, Dalla, and Williamson (2010, 579).

17. Månsson and Hedin (1999).

18. Baker, Dalla, and Williamson (2010).
19. Laub and Sampson (2003), and Sampson and Laub (1993).
20. See Britton (2000), Daly and Chesney-Lind (1988), and Giordano et al. (2006), among others.
21. Giordano, Cernkovich, and Rudolph (2002).
22. Giordano et al. (2002) use the phrase "hooks of change" to refer to the agency of the actor, who creatively and selectively appropriates elements in her environment (e.g., positive influence of a spouse) to serve as catalysts for identity shifts and long-term desistance.
23. Giordano (2010).
24. Matsueda and Heimer (1997), Uggen, Manza, and Behren (2004).
25. Howard (2006).
26. Ebaugh (1988).
27. Ebaugh (1988), Stryker (1980).
28. For further discussion of the relationship between the effects of stigma and role transitions, see Hagan and Wheaton (1993), Snow and Anderson (1987), Uggen, Manza, and Behren (2004).
29. Brown (1991).
30. Sanders (2007).
31. Kunda (2006).
32. Kunda (2006), Van Maanen (1976), Van Maanen and Schein (1979).
33. Van Maanen (1978), Van Maanen and Schein (1979).
34. Goffman (1961a), McCorkel (1998), Paterniti (2000), Ponticelli (1999).
35. In spite of their variation, I refer to all organizations whose purpose is to aid prostitutes as "prostitute-serving organizations."
36. Lofland et al. (2006).
37. The snowball sampling consisted of asking each PSO representative to name and provide information about any other PSOs in the United States. They often also named a contact person and a direct phone number where he or she could be reached. Because I could invoke another's recommendation, this strategy increased the odds that he or she would participate in the phone interview.
38. I assigned all four PSOs pseudonyms, as I promised to retain their anonymity in any published work that resulted from my research.
39. Dalla (2006), Ebaugh (1988), Goffman (1961a), Hanson (2002), and Kunda (2006).
40. Lofland et al. (2006).
41. Geertz (1973).
42. See Glaser and Strauss (1967) for a more detailed understanding of grounded theory.
43. Mishler (1986) and Punch (1986).

NOTES TO CHAPTER 2

1. See Shelley (2010) and Bales and Soodalter (2010) for recent analyses of sex trafficking.

2. For instance, see O'Connell Davidson (2005).
3. To read more about methodological concerns present within social science research on sex trafficking, see recent articles by Gozdziak (2012), Weitzer (2011), and Zhang (2009).
4. See Chin and Finckenauer (2012), Gozdziak (2012), and Mai (2011).
5. Chin and Finckenauer (2012, 235).
6. Certain scholars argue that all prostitution is involuntary, regardless of personal motivations or even when women claim to derive satisfaction from their performance, given that they are immersed within a patriarchal culture that exploits women and their sexuality (see Barry 1979, and Farley 2004).
7. Jennifer Cobbina and I advance a similar argument in an article published in *Sociological Inquiry* (2011). However, in that article, the analysis is based on data collected from female prisoners who worked as prostitutes (not affiliated with PSOs) *and* prostitutes immersed within PSOs. Unlike the article, the discussion in this book presents entrance pathways as a stage in the overall deviant career, and draws explicit connections between entrance types, experiences in prostitution, and initial exits into PSOs.
8. Brock (1998), Brody et al. (2005), Davis (2000), Hwang and Bedford (2003), Kramer and Berg (2003), Miller (1993), Raphael and Shapiro (2002), Rosen and Venkatesh (2008), and Simons and Whitbeck (1991).
9. Kramer and Berg (2003), and Miller (1986).
10. Davis (1971).
11. There is disagreement over the use of this term and its relationship to differential association theory (Sutherland 1939). While some argue the latter is actually a cultural deviance theory (Costello 1997), others point out this is a flawed misinterpretation of the theory (see Matsueda 1997).
12. Raphael and Shapiro (2002).
13. Brock (1998), Delacoste and Alexander (1998).
14. Rosen and Venkatesh (2008).
15. Epele (2001), and Porter and Bonilla (2010).
16. Gossop, Powes, Griffiths, and Strang (1994).
17. Cusick and Hickman (2005), Davis (2000).
18. Kramer and Berg (2003).
19. Laub and Sampson (2003), and Moffitt (1993).
20. Altogether, I excluded seven women from this chapter's analysis because I did not have sufficient information pertaining to their entry and time spent in the trade to categorize them.
21. Hayley and Gabriela partly fit into the first typology; however, they entered prostitution as adults rather than as adolescents. Although Jamilah entered prostitution as an adult and admits to having experimented with drugs recreationally when she was younger, she did not engage in prostitution to sustain a drug habit or to survive while on the streets.
22. Maher (1997), Inciardi et al. (1993), and Goldstein et al. (1992).

23. Maher (1997), and Williamson and Baker (2009).
24. Cusick and Hickman (2005).
25. Brock (1998), Miller (1986), Rosen and Venkatesh (2008), and Weitzer (2009b).
26. This measurement assesses initial exits from the trade to establish duration in sex work based upon their entrance into a PSO. Such placement, however, does not necessarily lead to long-term desistance.
27. Most women in this study stated that they had worked consistently in prostitution for the length of time they specified. However, there were some individuals who left for short durations of time—temporary breaks that were often attributed to other events such as being incarcerated, pregnant, in a hospital, or in a detox program. For the sake of this study, these calculations represent estimates of tenure in prostitution and are likely not exact measures. Rather, they constitute overall broad patterns and averages of time in the trade. Those who spent long periods of time working as prostitutes discussed the impact and salience of the factors that indicate a toll.
28. Barton (2006, 89).
29. Jody Miller (2008), Nikki Jones (2009), and Elijah Anderson (1999) all have generated commendable books examining urban violence among individuals (and youth) of color.
30. Miller (1995), Monto (2004), and Pearl (1987).
31. For exception, see Simpson, Yahner, and Dugan (2008).
32. Daly (1992, 1994).
33. Bernstein (2010).
34. In an article in *Sexualities*, Ron Weitzer and I (2013) examine the factors that prompt such advocacy among PSOs, and identify the various ways they perform it. Using an international analysis, Stephanie Limoncelli (2010) and others have also explored how social movements advance particular ideological stances that in turn shape policies regarding sex work and trafficking. In chapter 6 of this book, I further discuss the ways in which organizations and social movements are able to impact the laws and public perceptions that affect the lives of sex workers.
35. Dubyak (2012).
36. This pattern can also be found in other nondeviant careers, referred to as *burnout* in the organizational literature. For instance, see Maslach, Schaufeli, and Leiter (2001), and Schaufeli and Peeters (2000).

NOTES TO CHAPTER 3

1. Dalla (2000).
2. Dalla (2006), Månsson and Hedin (1999), and Sanders (2007).
3. For a more thorough discussion of these factors and how they differ from past studies on this topic, see Oselin (2010).
4. Review work by Dalla (2006) and Sanders (2007) for a discussion of these reasons.
5. Miller (1995), Monto (2004), Oselin and Blasyak (2013), Pearl (1987), and Raphael (2004).

6. To learn more about these strategies, refer to Oselin and Blasyak (2013).
7. Lofland and Stark (1965).
8. Månsson and Hedin (1999).
9. Sampson and Laub (1993).
10. Giordano, Deines, and Cernkovich (2006).
11. See Fernandez and Gould (1994).
12. Sociologist Helen Rose Ebaugh (1988) also stressed the importance of bridge parties to exiting roles generally, yet she focused primarily on the quantity and quality of the bridges as they related to happiness and adjustment after the exit was completed.

NOTES TO CHAPTER 4

1. Goffman (1961b, 108).
2. Goffman (1961b), Sayles (1984), and Snow and Anderson (1993).
3. Franks (2007), and Hochschild (2003).
4. Heatherton et al. (2000).
5. Goffman (1963).
6. Becker (1963).
7. Becker (1963).
8. Sanders (2007).
9. Turner (1962).
10. Snow and Anderson (1993).
11. Sayles (1984).
12. Franks (2007), and Hochschild (2003).
13. Van Maanen and Schein (1979, 230).
14. Goffman (1961a), and McCorkel (1998).
15. Ebaugh (1988).
16. Sanders (2007) also found that ex-sex workers indicated they wanted to be free from old social networks in order to avoid future deviance.
17. For more in-depth discussions of this argument, see Brock (1998), Jeffrey and MacDonald (2006), Miller (1986), and Rosen and Venkatesh (2008).
18. Goffman (1961a), McCorkel (1998), and Paterniti (2000).
19. In a historical analysis of UK programs, Judith Walkowitz (1980) acknowledges similar staff attempts to inculcate middle-class behaviors among Victorian-era prostitutes. However, she points out that such strategies were largely ineffective for generating change among this population.
20. Zaitzow and Thomas (2003).
21. Van Maanen (1978).
22. Van Maanen (1978).
23. See Chesney-Lind and Irwin (2008) for ostracism practiced among adolescent girls.
24. Kunda (2006) refers to this as "boundary passage."
25. Kunda (2006).

26. In contrast to my findings, family studies scholar Rochelle Dalla (2006) concludes that the type of exit (voluntary versus involuntary) significantly impacts the overall success of women leaving prostitution.

NOTES TO CHAPTER 5

1. Goffman (1961b, 106).
2. Drahota and Eitzen (1998), and Ebaugh (1988).
3. Sociologist Sheldon Stryker (1980) highlights the tight coupling between the roles we occupy and our identity.
4. Snow and Anderson (1987).
5. Vryan, Adler, and Adler (2003).
6. Berger and Luckmann (1967), Denzin (1987), Ponticelli (1999), Snow and Machalek (1984), and Travisano (1970).
7. Chapkis (1997), Lawless et al. (1996), and Pheterson (1996).
8. See Howard (2008).
9. Becker (1963).
10. Read Maruna (2001) for further discussion of this theory.
11. In her recent book, Peggy Giordano (2010) continues to argue that emotions can inform cognitive abilities, and that cognitions in turn are closely interrelated to identity formation processes.
12. Giordano, Cernkovich, and Rudolph (2002).
13. See Giordano et al. (2002, 1001).
14. To read more about the nuances of this argument, see Oselin (2009).
15. Arnold et al. (2000), and Porter and Bonilla (2010).
16. Brown (1991).
17. Sanders (2007).
18. Baker (2000), McCorkel (1998), and Schmid and Jones (1991).
19. For additional research on the relationship between social control mechanisms within institutional settings and identity changes, see Goffman (1961a), Horowitz (1995), McCorkel (1998), Paterniti (2000), and Silberman (1995).
20. Horowitz (1995).
21. Van Maanen and Schein (1979, 250).
22. Gardner (1978), Haenfler (2004), Hirsch (1990), and Kanter (1972).
23. Kanter (1972).
24. Haenfler (2004, 796).
25. Haenfler (2004) defines essential behaviors as prerequisites for group membership and collective identity; secondary behaviors were not required, yet indicated a higher level of commitment; and peripheral behaviors were rare, customized expressions of their collective identity. Although I do not assert that a collective identity existed among the prostitutes in this study, Haenfler's typology of behavior related to commitment is still applicable to the construction and displayed dedication to personal and social identities among my sample.

26. Cusick and Hickman (2005).
27. Lindsey (1997, 165).
28. Hill Collins (1987).
29. Walkowitz (1980).
30. To review this study and these findings, see Giordano et al. (2002).
31. To read more about this theory, see Ebaugh (1988).
32. Berger and Luckmann (1967).
33. Goffman (1961b), Matsueda and Heimer (1997), and Stryker (1980).
34. McAdam and Paulsen (1993).

NOTES TO CHAPTER 6

1. Read Baker et al. (2010) for a review of research on barriers to exiting street-level prostitution.
2. There are three main models that provide insight into the exiting process for female prostitutes. See Baker et al. (2010), Månsson and Hedin (1999), and Sanders (2007) to review them.
3. See Giordano and colleagues (2002) and Ebaugh (1988), respectively, for an elaboration of these theories.
4. Giordano et al. (2002, 999).
5. Dalla (2006), and Sanders (2007).
6. The remaining 7.5 percent did not answer this question with sufficient information.
7. Baker et al. (2010), Ebaugh (1988), and Mansson and Hedin (1999).
8. See Ebaugh (1988).
9. Maruna (2001).
10. Denzin (1987), Snow and Machalek (1984), and Taylor (1996).
11. The educational attainment for two women in this sample is unknown.
12. In this study Peggy Giordano and colleagues (2002) do not focus specifically on prostitutes, but rather on a variety of female offenders.
13. Becker (1960), and Ebaugh (1988).
14. John Van Maanen and Edgar Schein (1979, 252).
15. Sanders (2007).
16. Farley and Kelly (2000), Jeffreys (1997), and Pateman (1988).
17. Chapkis (1997), and Delacoste and Alexander (1998).
18. Bernstein (2007), Dewey (2010), Sanders (2005), and Weitzer (2010).
19. In a related vein, another model has been implemented in Sweden that decriminalizes working in prostitution but instead criminalizes buying sex. So the punitive target has shifted from worker to client, based on interventionist efforts to pull women out of prostitution and dampen demand. This law passed in 1999 and has since been adopted by a few other countries, such as Norway and Iceland. To read more about the Swedish model, see Månsson and Hedin (1999) or Waltman (2012).

20. For a more thorough discussion, see Brents, Jackson, and Hausbeck (2010), and Weitzer (2012).
21. Ronald Weitzer (1999) argues the United States uses this approach.
22. Scott (2001) and Weitzer (1999).
23. Brents, Jackson, and Hausbeck (2010).
24. Weitzer (2012).
25. Brents, Jackson, and Hausbeck (2010).
26. Monto (2004).
27. For example, a Chicago Police Department webpage showcases the arrests of individuals charged with solicitation by posting their pictures. See https://portal.chicagopolice.org/portal/page/portal/ClearPath/Online%20Services/Prostitution%20Arrests.
28. Sociologist Martin Monto (2004) analyzes the variety of punishments directed at male customers of prostitutes, including public shaming practices and john schools.
29. Dalla (2006).
30. For a more in-depth discussion of punitive practices directed at customers, see Ronald Weitzer's book, *Legalizing Prostitution*, (2012, 67–68).
31. Weitzer (2012).
32. Sociologist Deborah Brock (1998) uncovers this pattern of relocation among street prostitutes in Toronto, Canada.
33. Brock (1998), Jeffrey and MacDonald (2006), Miller (1986), and Sanders (2007).
34. Rochelle Dalla (2006, 143).
35. Of the 29 PSOs, there are five that are either exclusively devoted to youth engaged in prostitution, or serve both adolescent and adult prostitutes. The rest offer services intended for adult sex workers.
36. For exceptions, see the following works by Bjønness (2012), Jenness (1993), Limoncelli (2006, 2010), and Majic (2011).
37. Limoncelli (2006).
38. Bjønness (2012).
39. See Chapkis (1997) and Jenness (1993) for detailed examinations of social movements focused on prostitution and sex work.
40. This is a simplistic rendering of the arguments present in our article. For an in-depth analysis, see Oselin and Weitzer (2013) in *Sexualities*.
41. Majic (2011).
42. Dalla (2000).

NOTES TO THE METHODOLOGICAL APPENDIX
1. Mazzei and O'Brien (2009).
2. Glaser and Strauss (1967).
3. Kunda (2006, 23).

REFERENCES

Aggleton, Peter (ed.). 1999. *Men Who Sell Sex.* Philadelphia: Temple University Press.

Alexander, Priscilla. 1998. "Prostitution: A Difficult Issue for Feminists." In *Sex Work: Writings by Women in the Sex Industry*, edited by F. Delacoste and P. Alexander, 184–214. Berkeley, CA: Cleis Press.

Anderson, Elijah. 1999. *Code of the Street: Decency, Violence and the Moral Life of the Inner City.* New York: Norton.

Arnold, Elizabeth M., J. Chris Stewart, and C. Aaron McNeece. 2000. "The Psychosocial Treatment Needs of Street-Walking Prostitutes: Perspectives from a Case Management Program." *Journal of Offender Rehabilitation* 30(3–4): 117–32.

Baker, Lynda, Rochelle Dalla, and Celia Williamson. 2010. "Exiting Prostitution: An Integrated Model." *Violence Against Women* 16(5): 579–600.

Baker, Phyllis. 2000. "I Didn't Know: Discoveries and Identity Transformation of Women Addicts in Treatment." *Journal of Drug Issues* 30(4): 863–80.

Bales, Kevin, and Ron Soodalter. 2010 (2nd edition). *The Slave Next Door: Human Trafficking and Slavery in America Today.* Berkeley: University of California Press.

Barry, Kathleen. 1979. *Female Sexual Slavery.* New York: Avon Books.

Barton, Bernadette. 2006. *Stripped: Inside the Lives of Exotic Dancers.* New York: New York University Press.

Becker, Howard. 1960. "Notes on the Concept of Commitment." *American Journal of Sociology* 66(1): 32–44.

Becker, Howard. 1963. *Outsiders: Studies in the Sociology of Deviance.* New York: Free Press.

Berger, Peter, and Thomas Luckmann. 1967. *The Social Construction of Reality: A Treatise in the Sociology of Knowledge.* Garden City, NY: Doubleday.

Bernstein, Elizabeth. 2007. *Temporarily Yours: Intimacy, Authenticity, and the Commerce of Sex.* Chicago: University of Chicago Press.

Bernstein, Elizabeth. 2010. "Militarized Humanitarianism Meets Carceral Feminism: The Politics of Sex, Rights, and Freedom in Contemporary Antitrafficking Campaigns." *Signs: Journal of Women in Culture and Society* 36(1): 45–71.

Bjønness, Jeanett. 2012. "Between Emotional Politics and Biased Practices—Prostitution Policies, Social Work, and Women Selling Sexual Services in Denmark." *Sexuality Research and Social Policy* 9(3):192–202.

Bourgois, P., and E. Dunlap. 1993. "Exorcising Sex-For-Crack: An Ethnographic Perspective from Harlem." In *Crack Pipe as Pimp: An Ethnographic Investigation of Sex-For-Crack Exchanges*, edited by M. S. Ratner, 97–132. New York: Lexington.

Brents, Barbara, Crystal A. Jackson, and Kathryn Hausbeck. 2010. *The State of Sex: Tourism, Sex, and Sin in the New American Heartland.* New York: Routledge.

Britton, Dana. 2000. "Feminism in Criminology: Engendering the Outlaw." *Annals of the American Academy of Political and Social Science* 571(1): 57–76.

Brock, Deborah. 1998. *Making Work, Making Trouble: Prostitution as a Social Problem.* Toronto: University of Toronto Press.

Brody, Stuart, John J. Potterat, Stephen Q. Muth, and Donald E. Woodhouse. 2005. "Psychiatric and Characterological Factors Relevant to Excess Mortality in a Long-Term Cohort of Prostitute Women." *Journal of Sex and Marital Therapy* 31(2): 97–112.

Brown, J. David. 1991. "The Professional Ex-: An Alternative for Exiting the Deviant Career." *Sociological Quarterly* 32(2): 219–30.

Chapkis, Wendy. 1997. *Live Sex Acts: Women Performing Erotic Labor.* New York: Routledge.

Chapkis, Wendy. 2000. "Power and Control in the Commercial Sex Trade." In *Sex for Sale*, edited by R. Weitzer, 181–201. New York: Routledge.

Chesney-Lind, Meda, and Katherine Irwin. 2008. *Beyond Bad Girls: Gender, Violence and Hype.* New York: Routledge.

Chin, Ko-Lin, and James Finckenauer. 2012. *Selling Sex Overseas: Chinese Women and the Realities of Prostitution and Global Sex Trafficking.* New York: New York University Press.

Cobbina, Jennifer, and Sharon S. Oselin. 2011. "It's Not Only for the Money: An Analysis of Adolescent versus Adult Entry into Street Prostitution" *Sociological Inquiry* 81(3): 1–24.

Collins, Patricia Hill. 1987. "The Meaning of Motherhood in Black Culture and Black Mother-Daughter Relationships" *Sage: A Scholarly Journal on Black Women* 4(2): 4–11.

Costello, Barbara. 1997. "On the Logical Adequacy of Cultural Deviance Theories." *Theoretical Criminology* 1(4): 403–28.

Cusick, Linda, and Matthew Hickman. 2005. "'Trapping' in Drug Use and Sex Work Careers." *Drugs: Education, Prevention and Policy* 12(5): 369–79.

Dalla, Rochelle. 2000. "Exposing the 'Pretty Woman' Myth: A Qualitative Examination of the Lives of Female Streetwalking Prostitutes." *Journal of Sex Research* 37(4): 344–66.

Dalla, Rochelle. 2006. *Exposing the "Pretty Woman" Myth: A Qualitative Investigation of Street Level Prostituted Women.* Lanham, MD: Lexington.

Daly, Kathleen. 1992. "Women's Pathways to Felony Court: Feminist Theories of Lawbreaking and Problems of Representation." *Southern California Review of Law and Women's Studies* 2(1): 11–52.

Daly, Kathleen. 1994. *Gender, Crime, and Punishment.* New Haven, CT: Yale University Press.

Daly, Kathleen, and Meda Chesney-Lind. 1988. "Feminism and Criminology." *Justice Quarterly* 5(4): 497–538.

Davis, Nanette. 1971. "The Prostitute: Developing a Deviant Identity." In *Studies in the Sociology of Sex,* edited by J. M. Henslin, 297–322. New York: Appleton-Century-Crofts.

Davis, Nanette. 2000. "From Victims to Survivors: Working with Recovering Street Prostitutes." In *Sex for Sale,* edited by Ronald Weitzer, 139–55. New York: Routledge.

Delacoste, Frederique, and Priscilla Alexander. 1998. *Sex Work: Writings by Women in the Sex Industry.* Berkeley, CA: Cleis Press.

Denzin, Norman K. 1987. *The Recovering Alcoholic.* Thousand Oaks, CA: Sage.

Dewey, Susan. 2010. *Neon Wasteland: On Love, Motherhood, and Sex Work in a Rust Belt Town.* Berkeley: University of California Press.

Drahota, Jo Anne Tremaine, and D. Stanley Eitzen. 1998. "The Role Exit of Professional Athletes." *Sociology of Sport Journal* 15(3): 263–78.

Dubyak, Erin. 2012. "'Flying the Plane as We Build It': A Qualitative Study of an Organization's Goals and Actions toward the Prevention of Exploited Female Youth." Unpublished master's thesis, Oregon State University.

Ebaugh, Helen Rose Fuchs. 1988. *Becoming an Ex: The Process of Role Exit.* Chicago: University of Chicago Press.

Epele, MarÕa. 2001. "Excess, Scarcity & Desire Among Drug-Using Sex Workers." *Body and Society* 7(2–3): 161–79.

Farley, Melissa. 2004. "'Bad for the Body, Bad for the Heart': Prostitution Harms Women Even If Legalized or Decriminalized." *Violence Against Women* 10(10): 1087–125.

Farley, Melissa, and Vanessa Kelly. 2000. "Prostitution: A Critical Review of the Medical and Social Sciences Literature." *Women and Criminal Justice* 11(4): 29–64.

Fernandez, Roberto M., and Roger V. Gould. 1994. "A Dilemma of State Power: Brokerage and Influence in the National Health Policy Domain." *American Journal of Sociology* 99(6): 1455–91.

Forbes, A. 1993. "Crack Cocaine and HIV: How National Drug-Addiction Treatment Deficits Fan the Pandemic's Flame." *AIDS & Public Policy Journal* 8(1): 44–52.

Franks, David D. 2007. "Role." In *Blackwell Encyclopedia of Sociology Online,* edited by George Ritzer. Hoboken, NJ: Blackwell-Wiley. http://www.blackwellreference.com/public/tocnode?id=g9781405124331_yr2012_chunk_g978140512433124_ss1-76#citation.

Gardner, John. 1978. *The Children of Prosperity: Thirteen Modern American Communes.* New York: St. Martin's Press.

Geertz, Clifford. 1973. "Thick Description: Toward an Interpretive Theory of Culture." In *The Interpretation of Culture,* edited by C. Geertz, 3–30. New York: Basic Books.

Giordano, Peggy C. 2010. *Legacies of Crime: A Follow-Up of the Children of Highly Delinquent Girls and Boys.* New York: Cambridge University Press.

Giordano, Peggy C., Stephen A. Cernkovich, and Jennifer L. Rudolph. 2002. "Gender, Crime and Desistance: Toward a Cognitive Theory of Transformation." *American Journal of Sociology* 107(4): 990–1064.

Giordano, Peggy C., Jill A. Deines, and Stephen A. Cernkovich. 2006. "In and Out of Crime: A Life Course Perspective on Girls' Delinquency." In *Gender and Crime: Patterns in Victimization and Offending*, edited by Karen Heimer and Candace Kruttschnitt, 17–40. New York: New York University Press.

Glaser, Barney, and Anselm Strauss. 1967. *The Discovery of Grounded Theory: Strategies for Qualitative Research.* Chicago: Aldine.

Goldstein, P. J., L. J. Ouellet, and M. Fendrich. 1992. "From Bag Brides to Skeezers: A Historical Perspective on Sex-For-Drugs Behavior." *Journal of Psychoactive Drugs* 24(4): 349–61.

Goffman, Erving. 1961a. *Asylums: Essays on the Social Situation of Mental Patients and Other Inmates.* Garden City, NY: Anchor.

Goffman, Erving. 1961b. *Encounters: Two Studies in the Sociology of Interaction—Fun in Games & Role Distance.* Indianapolis, IN: Bobbs-Merrill.

Goffman, Erving. 1963. *Stigma: Notes on the Management of Spoiled Identity.* Englewood Cliffs, NJ: Prentice Hall.

Gossop, Michael, Beverly Powes, Paul Griffiths, and John Strang. 1994. "Sexual Behavior and Its Relationship to Drug-Taking among Prostitutes in South London." *Addiction* 89(8): 961–70.

Gozdziak, Elzbieta. 2012. "Children Trafficked to the United States: Myths and Realities." *Global Dialogue* 14(2): 51–61.

Haenfler, Ross. 2004. "Collective Identity in the Straight Edge Movement: How Diffuse Movements Foster Commitment, Encourage Individualized Participation, and Promote Cultural Change." *Sociological Quarterly* 45(4): 785–805.

Hagan, John, and Blair Wheaton. 1993. "The Search for Adolescent Role Exits and the Transition to Adulthood." *Social Forces* 71(4): 955–79.

Hanson, Glen R. 2002. "Therapeutic Community." *National Institute on Drug Abuse Research Report*: Washington, DC: US Department of Health and Human Services.

Heatherton, T. F., R. E. Kleck, M. Hebl, and J. G. Hull, (eds.) 2000. *The Social Psychology of Stigma.* New York: Guilford Press.

Hirsch, Eric L. 1990. "Sacrifice for the Cause: Group Processes, Recruitment, and Commitment in a Student Social Movement." *American Sociological Review* 55(2): 243–54.

Hochschild, Arlie Russell. 2003. *The Commercialization of Intimate Life: Notes From Home and Work.* Berkeley: University of California Press.

Horowitz, Ruth. 1995. *Teen Mothers—Citizens or Dependents?* Chicago: University of Chicago.

Howard, Jenna. 2006. "Expecting and Accepting: The Temporal Ambiguity of Recovery Identities." *Social Psychology Quarterly* 69(4): 307–24.

Howard, Jenna. 2008. "Negotiating an Exit: Existential, Interactional, and Cultural Obstacles to Disorder Disidentification." *Social Psychology Quarterly* 71(2): 177–92.

Hwang, Shu-Ling, and Olwen Bedford. 2003. "Precursors and Pathways to Juvenile Prostitution in Taiwan." *Journal of Sex Research* 40(2): 201–10.

Inciardi, J. A., D. Lockwood, and A. E. Pottieger. 1993. *Women and Crack Cocaine.* New York: Macmillan.

Jeffrey, Leslie A., and Gayle MacDonald. 2006. "'It's the Money, Honey': The Economy of Sex Work in the Maritimes." *Canadian Review of Sociology and Anthropology* 43(3): 313–27.

Jeffreys, Sheila. 1997. *The Idea of Prostitution.* North Melbourne, Australia: Spinifex.

Jenness, Valerie. 1993. *Making it Work: The Prostitutes' Rights Movement in Perspective.* New York: Aldine de Gruyter.

Jones, Nikki. 2009. *Between Good and Ghetto: African American Girls and Inner-City Violence.* New Brunswick, NJ: Rutgers University Press.

Kaye, Kerwin. 2003. "Male Prostitution in the Twentieth Century: Pseudo Homosexuals, Hoodlum Homosexuals, and Exploited Teens." *Journal of Homosexuality* 46(1–2): 1–77.

Kanter, Rosabeth. 1972. *Commitment and Community: Communes and Utopias in Sociological Perspective.* Cambridge, MA: Harvard University Press.

Kramer, Lisa A., and Ellen C. Berg. 2003. "A Survival Analysis of Timing of Entry into Prostitution: The Differential Impact of Race, Educational Level, and Childhood/ Adolescent Risk Factors." *Sociological Inquiry* 73(4): 511–28.

Kunda, Gideon. 2006. *Engineering Culture: Control and Commitment in a High-Tech Corporation* (rev. edition). Philadelphia, PA: Temple University Press.

Laub, John H., and Robert J. Sampson. 2003. *Shared Beginnings, Divergent Lives: Delinquent Boys to Age 70.* Cambridge, MA: Harvard University Press.

Lawless, Sonia, Susan Kippax, and June Crawford. 1996. "Dirty, Diseased and Undeserving: The Positioning of HIV Positive Women." *Social Science and Medicine* 43(9): 1370–77.

Limoncelli, Stephanie A. 2006. "International Voluntary Associations, Local Social Movements and State Paths to the Abolition of Regulated Prostitution in Europe, 1875–1950." *International Sociology* 21(1):31–59.

Limoncelli, Stephanie A. 2010. *The Politics of Trafficking: The First International Movement to Combat the Sexual Exploitation of Women.* Stanford, CA: Stanford University Press.

Lindsey, Linda L. 1997. *Gender Roles: A Sociological Perspective* (3rd edition). Upper Saddle River, NJ: Prentice-Hall.

Lofland, John, David Snow, Leon Anderson, and Lyn Lofland. 2006. *Analyzing Social Settings: A Guide to Qualitative Observation and Analysis.* Belmont, CA: Thomson/ Wadsworth.

Lofland, John, and Rodney Stark. 1965. "Becoming a World-Saver: A Theory of Conversion to a Deviant Perspective." *American Sociological Review* 30(6): 862–75.

Maher, Lisa. 1997. *Sexed Work: Gender, Race, and Resistance in a Brooklyn Drug Market.* New York: Oxford University Press.

Mai, Nick. 2011. "Tampering with the Sex of 'Angels': Migrant Male Minors and Young Adults Selling Sex in the EU." *Journal of Ethnic and Migration Studies* 37(8): 1237–52.

Majic, Samantha. 2011. "Serving Sex Workers and Promoting Democratic Engagement: Re-thinking Nonprofits' Role in American Civic and Political Life." *Perspectives on Politics* 9(4): 821–40.

Månsson, Sven-Axel, and Ulla-Carin Hedin. 1999. "Breaking the Matthew Effect—On Women Leaving Prostitution." *International Journal of Social Welfare* 8(1): 67–77.

Maruna, Shadd. 2001. *Making Good: How Ex-Convicts Reform and Rebuild their Lives.* Washington, DC: American Psychological Association.

Maslach, Christina, Wilmar B. Schaufeli, and Michael P. Leiter. 2001. "Job Burnout." *Annual Review of Psychology* 52(1): 397–422.

Matsueda, Ross, and Karen Heimer. 1997. "A Symbolic Interactionist Theory of Role-Transitions, Role-Commitments, and Delinquency." In *Developmental Theories of Crime and Delinquency*, edited by Terence P. Thornberry, 163–213. New Brunswick, NJ: Transaction Publishers.

Matsueda, Ross. 1997. "'Cultural Deviance Theory': The Remarkable Persistence of a Flawed Term." *Theoretical Criminology* 1(4): 429–52.

Mazzei, Julie, and Erin E. O'Brien. 2009. "You Got It, So When Do You Flaunt It?: Building Rapport, Intersectionality, and the Strategic Deployment of Gender in the Field." *Journal of Contemporary Ethnography* 38(3): 358–83.

McAdam, Doug, and Ronnelle Paulsen. 1993. "Specifying the Relationship between Social Ties and Activism." In *Social Movements: Readings on Their Emergence, Mobilization, and Dynamics,* edited by Doug McAdam and David A. Snow, 145–57. Los Angeles: Roxbury Publishing Company.

McCorkel, Jill. 1998. "Going to the Crackhouse: Critical Space as a Form of Resistance in Total Institutions and Everyday Life." *Symbolic Interaction* 21(3): 227–52.

Miller, Eleanor. 1986. *Street Woman.* Philadelphia, PA: Temple University Press.

Miller, Jody. 1993. "Your Life is on the Line Every Night You're on the Streets: Victimization and the Resistance Among Street Prostitutes." *Humanity & Society* 17(4): 422–46.

Miller, Jody. 1995. "Gender and Power on the Streets: Street Prostitution in the Era of Crack Cocaine." *Journal of Contemporary Ethnography* 23(4): 427–52.

Miller, Jody. 2008. *Getting Played: African American Girls, Urban Inequality, and Gendered Violence.* New York: New York University Press.

Mishler, Elliot G. 1986. *Research Interviewing: Context and Narrative.* Cambridge, MA: Harvard University Press.

Moffitt, Terrie E. 1993. "The Neuropsychology of Conduct Disorder." *Development and Psychopathology* 5(1–2): 135–52.

Monto, Martin. 2004. "Female Prostitutes, Customers, and Violence." *Violence Against Women* 10(2): 160–88.

Murphy, Alexandra K., and Sudhir Alladi Venkatesh. 2006. "Vice Careers: The Changing Contours of Sex Work in New York City." *Qualitative Sociology* 29(2): 129–54.

O'Connell Davidson, Julia. 2005. *Children in the Global Sex Trade*. Cambridge, UK: Polity Press.

Oselin, Sharon S. 2009. "Leaving the Streets: Transformation of Prostitute Identity Within the Prostitution Rehabilitation Program." *Deviant Behavior* 30(4): 379–406.

Oselin, Sharon S. 2010. "Weighing the Consequences of a Deviant Career: Motivations and Opportunities for Leaving Prostitution." *Sociological Perspectives* 53(4): 527–49.

Oselin, Sharon S., and Aaron Blasyak. 2013. "Contending with Violence: Female Prostitutes' Strategic Responses on the Streets." *Deviant Behavior* 3(4): 274–90.

Oselin, Sharon S., and Ronald Weitzer. 2013. "Organizations Working on Behalf of Prostitutes: An Analysis of Goals, Practices and Strategies." *Sexualities* 16(3-4): 445–66.

Pateman, Carole. 1988. *The Sexual Contract*. Stanford, CA: Stanford University Press.

Paterniti, Debora. 2000. "The Micropolitics of Identity in Adverse Circumstance." *Journal of Contemporary Ethnography* 29(1): 93–119.

Pearl, Julie. 1987. "The Highest Paying Customers: America's Cities and the Costs of Prostitution Control." *Hastings Law Journal* 38(4): 769–800.

Pheterson, Gail. 1996. *The Prostitution Prism*. Amsterdam: Amsterdam University.

Ponticelli, Christy. 1999. "Crafting Stories of Sexual Identity Reconstruction." *Social Psychology Quarterly* 62(2): 157–72.

Porter, Judith, and Louis Bonilla. 2010. "Drug Use, HIV, and the Ecology of Street Prostitution." In *Sex for Sale* (2nd edition), edited by R. Weitzer, 163–86. New York: Routledge.

Potterat, John J., Richard B. Rothenberg, Stephen Q. Muth, William W. Darrow, and Lynanne Phillips-Plummer. 1998. "Pathways to Prostitution: The Chronology of Sexual and Drug Abuse Milestones." *Journal of Sex Research* 35(4): 333–40.

Punch, Maurice. 1986. *The Politics and Ethics of Fieldwork*. Thousand Oaks, CA: Sage.

Raphael, Jody. 2004. *Listening to Olivia: Violence, Poverty, and Prostitution*. Boston: Northeastern University Press.

Raphael, Jody, and Deborah Shapiro. 2002. "Sisters Speak Out: The Lives and Needs of Prostituted Women in Chicago." Chicago: Center for Impact Research Report.

Rosen, Eva, and Sudhir Alladi Venkatesh. 2008. "A Perversion of Choice: Sex Work Offers Just Enough in Chicago's Urban Ghetto." *Journal of Contemporary Ethnography* 37(4): 417–41.

Sampson, Robert J., and John H. Laub. 1993. *Crime in the Making: Pathways and Turning Points through Life*. Cambridge, MA: Harvard University Press.

Sanders, Teela. 2005. *Sex Work: A Risky Business*. Cullompton, UK: Willan.

Sanders, Teela. 2007. "Becoming an Ex-Sex Worker: Making Transitions Out of a Deviant Career." *Feminist Criminology* 2(1): 74–95.

Sayles, Marnie. 1984. "Role Distancing: Differentiating the Role of the Elderly from the Person." *Qualitative Sociology* 7(3): 236–52.

Schaufeli, Wilmar B., and Maria C. W. Peeters. 2000. "Job Stress and Burnout Among Correctional Officers: A Literature Review." *International Journal of Stress Management* 7(1): 19–48.

Schmid, Thomas J., and Richard S. Jones. 1991. "Suspended Identity: Identity Transformation in a Maximum Security Prison." *Symbolic Interaction* 14(4): 415–32.

Scott, Michael. 2001. *Street Prostitution*. Washington, DC: US Department of Justice.

Seng, Magnus J. 1989. "Child Sexual Abuse and Adolescent Prostitution: A Comparative Analysis." *Adolescence* 24(95): 665–75.

Shelley, Louise. 2010. *Human Trafficking: A Global Perspective*. New York: Cambridge University Press.

Silberman, Matthew. 1995. *A World of Violence: Corrections in America*. Belmont, CA: Wadsworth.

Simons, Ronald L., and Les B. Witbeck. 1991. "Sexual Abuse as a Precursor to Prostitution and Victimization among Adolescent and Adult Homeless Women." *Journal of Family Issues* 12(3): 361–79.

Simpson, Sally S., Jennifer L. Yahner, and Laura Dugan. 2008. "Understanding Women's Pathways to Jail: Analysing the Lives of Incarcerated Women." *Australian and New Zealand Journal of Criminology* 41(4): 84–108.

Snow, David A., and Leon Anderson. 1987. "Identity Work Among the Homeless: The Verbal Construction and Avowal of Personal Identities." *American Journal of Sociology* 92(6): 1336–71.

Snow, David A., and Leon Anderson. 1993. *Down on their Luck: A Study of Homeless Street People*. Berkeley: University of California Press.

Snow, David A., and Richard Machalek. 1984. "The Sociology of Conversion." *Annual Review of Sociology* 10: 167–90.

Stryker, Sheldon. 1980. *Symbolic Interactionism: A Social Structural Version*. Menlo Park, CA: Benjamin-Cummings.

Sutherland, Edwin H. 1939. *Principles of Criminology*. Philadelphia, PA: Lippincott.

Taylor, Verta. 1996. *Rock-a-by Baby: Feminism, Self-Help, and Postpartum Depression*. New York: Routledge.

Travisano, Richard V. 1970. "Alternation and Conversion as Qualitatively Different Transformations." In *Social Psychology through Symbolic Interaction*, edited by Gregory P. Stone and Harvey A. Farberman, 594–606. Waltham, MA: Ginn-Blaisdell.

Turner, Ralph. 1962. "Role-Taking: Process Versus Conformity." In *Human Behavior and Social Processes*, edited by A. M. Rose, 20–40. Boston: Houghton Mifflin.

Uggen, Christopher, Jeff Manza, and Angela Behren. 2004. "Less than the Average Citizen: Stigma, Role Transition, and the Civic Reintegration of Convicted Felons." In *After Crime and Punishment: Pathways to Offender Reintegration*, edited by Shadd Maruna and Russ Immarigeon, 258–90. Devon, UK: Willan Publishing.

US Department of Justice. 2001. "The Sex Trafficking of Women in the United States." Washington, DC: US Office of Justice Programs.

Van Maanen, John. 1976. "Breaking In: Socialization to Work." In *Handbook of Work, Organizations, and Society*, edited by Robert Dubin, 67–130. Chicago: Rand McNally.

Van Maanen, John. 1978. "People Processing: Strategies of Organizational Socialization." *Organizational Dynamics* 7(1): 18–36.

Van Maanen, John, and Edgar H. Schein. 1979. "Toward a Theory of Organizational Socialization." In *Research in Organizational Behavior* (Vol. 1), edited by Barry Staw, 209–69. Greenwich, CT: JAI Press.

Vryan, Kevin D., Patricia A. Adler, and Peter Adler. 2003. "Identity." In *Handbook of Symbolic Interactionism*, edited by Larry Reynolds and Nancy Herman, 367–90. Walnut Creek, CA: AltaMira Press.

Walkowitz, Judith. 1980. *Prostitution and Victorian Society: Women, Class and the State*. New York: Cambridge University Press.

Waltman, Max. 2012. "Criminalize Only the Buying of Sex." *New York Times*, April 20. www.nytimes.com/roomfordebate/2012/04/19/is-legalized-prostitution-safer/criminalize-buying-not-selling-sex.

Weitzer, Ronald. 1999. "Prostitution Control in America: Rethinking Public Policy." *Crime, Law and Social Change* 32(1): 83–102.

Weitzer, Ronald. 2000. "Why We Need More Research on Sex Work." In *Sex for Sale*, edited by R. Weitzer, 1–13. New York: Routledge.

Weitzer, Ronald. 2009a. "Legalizing Prostitution: Morality Politics in Western Australia." *British Journal of Criminology* 49(1): 88–105.

Weitzer, Ronald. 2009b. "Sociology of Sex Work." *Annual Review of Sociology* 35(1): 213–34.

Weitzer, Ronald. 2010. "Sex Work: Paradigms and Policies." In *Sex for Sale* (2nd edition), edited by R. Weitzer, 1–43. New York: Routledge.

Weitzer, Ronald. 2011. "Sex Trafficking and the Sex Industry: The Need for Evidence-Based Theory and Legislation." *Journal of Criminal Law & Criminology* 101(4): 1337–70.

Weitzer, Ronald. 2012. Legalizing Prostitution: From Illicit Vice to Lawful Business. New York: New York University Press.

West, Donald. 1993. *Male Prostitution*. Binghamton, NY: Haworth.

Whelehan, Patricia. 2001. *An Anthropological Perspective on Prostitution: The World's Oldest Profession*. Lewiston, NY: Edwin Mellen Press.

Williamson, Celia, and Lynda M. Baker. 2009. "Women in Street-Based Prostitution: A Typology of their Work Styles." *Qualitative Social Work* 8(1): 27–44.

Zaitzow, Barbara, and Jim Thomas. 2003. *Women in Prison: Gender and Social Control*. Boulder, CO: Lynne Reinner.

Zhang, Sheldon. 2009. "Beyond the 'Natasha' Story—A Review and Critique of Current Research on Sex Trafficking." *Global Crime* 10(3): 178–95.

INDEX

ABOUT THE AUTHOR

Sharon S. Oselin is an Assistant Professor in the Department of Sociology at California State University, Los Angeles.